THE SPORTS BUCKET LIST

THE SPORTS BUCKET LIST

101

SIGHTS EVERY FAN HAS TO SEE BEFORE THE CLOCK RUNS OUT

WRITTEN AND EDITED BY **ROB FLEDER**

CREATIVE DIRECTION BY **STEVE HOFFMAN**

PHOTO EDITING BY **DOT McMAHON**

HARPER
DESIGN

An Imprint of HarperCollinsPublishers

THE SPORTS BUCKET LIST

INTRODUCTION

BY ROB FLEDER

As an anonymous sports fan once said, "Life is not measured by the number of breaths we take, but by the places and moments that take our breath away." I don't actually know if the guy who said that was a sports fan (or a guy, for that matter), but I do know that, for those of us who love sports, the thrill of seeing an epic event or a storied arena is something close to the meaning of life. The voltage that runs through the crowd before the first pitch or the opening tip- or face-off of game seven—any game seven; the buzz of anticipation that fills the arena in the minutes before a heavyweight title fight; the insane, raucous energy unleashed in Cameron Indoor Arena as Duke takes the floor against Carolina; the palpable current that surges through an Olympic stadium as the sprinters coil into the starting blocks for the 100-meter finals: for a sports fan, this is what it's all about.

WE ARE ALL THRILL SEEKERS and memory collectors (memory hoarders, even, if I am in any way typical; my brain is stuffed with all sorts of sports junk—opinions, recollections, facts that will probably never come to light again and are of no further use, though I hold on to all of them and accumulate more every day). As we check items off our bucket lists, those checks

Before you knew it, LeBron the rookie phenom …

are mementos, and the lists are the scrapbooks of all the places we've been and the games we've seen. But the list isn't just historical, it's aspirational—a to-do list, a note to ourselves about our agenda, an impatiently tapping toe: time's a-wastin'. What are we waiting for?

TAKE A QUICK GLANCE at the bucket list in this book and you'll notice that the items fall into three distinct categories: those that focus on people (individuals or teams), on places, and on events. The aim here is to cover a broad spectrum of sports and the widest possible sweep of geography. It is the nature of any bucket list to be personal and subjective—and therefore inherently debatable. What we've tried to do is preserve the passion and personal preference at the heart of such a list while creating one that, based on our decades of experience as sports journalists covering and attending events, will be useful to all kinds of fans. We could've easily made a list that included nothing but rivalry games between Division 1 college football teams, for instance, each crackling with its history of triumphs and grudges, and charged anew each year with expectation and pressure. Instead, we chose to include a much wider range of sports and just a few exemplary rivalry games (huge football games that by any measure belong on every fan's list).

BY THE SAME TOKEN, you might notice events or places that strike you as conspicuous by their absence here, but rest assured that nothing obvious was omitted without deliberation. The World Series, for instance, is not on this list, though I have attended Series games in various cities and collected memories there that I wouldn't trade for a club-level Super Bowl ticket

(Reggie Jackson's three home runs on consecutive pitches in Game 6 against the Dodgers in 1977? Check. Kirk Gibson's pinch-hit walk-off fist-pump homer against the A's in '88? Check.) But interleague play has neutralized some of the thrill that used to attach to the Series when it was the only chance to see National and American League teams meet (All-Star exhibitions notwithstanding). And it's an event you really want to see *your* team play in; even if you're a serious baseball fan, would Game 2 of, say, a Twins-Padres Series, make your life feel more complete? Finally, no one can predict, till a couple days before it starts, when or where the World Series will be. If the stars align, you have to be ready, on the spur of the moment, to pounce. But then, you don't need our list to tell you that. It's a game of opportunity, and that's also why our list is not ranked. We add items to our list when the need becomes irresistible, and we check them off whenever we possibly can. What's important is seeing the people and places and events, not trying to do the impossible by dictating the order in which they should be seen.

THE FLIP SIDE OF LEAVING out a few obvious items is including a few that might strike you at first as odd. I can almost hear the heckler now: Elephant polo? What's that all about? To which I can only say: Who wouldn't want to see guys ride around on stampeding pachyderms, chasing a little ball and whacking at it with incredibly long mallets, trying to knock it into a goal? And though the intention here is to be mostly realistic, to include events and places you might reasonably hope to see, I believe that any decent wish list ought to include some wishes that aren't odds-on to come true. Maybe you don't have to summit Mount Everest, but wouldn't you like to get close enough to try?

DURING THE TIME it took to assemble this bucket list, another kind of reminder kept popping up, the kind that marks, in sports terms, the passage of large chunks of time: the appearance of an old player's obituary, or the retirement of a player I realized I'd watched as a kid breaking in, as a rising star, as a prime-time player, and as a trusty veteran; a player I'd watched for his entire career, from beginning to end. Sure, there will always be another season, but the long good-byes of Derek Jeter and Kobe Bryant, the last postseason bows of Peyton Manning and Tim Duncan, and the final bell for Muhammad Ali and Gordie Howe should remind every fan that "wait till next year," while often consoling, is not always the best advice we can give ourselves. When a new stadium opens and they tear down the old one, remember that the urgency of a bucket list comes not just from our own ticking clock, but also from the buzzer that sounds on teams and leagues, on buildings and athletic careers.

...was the NBA's venerable King James.

THE BEST WAY TO SEE all those athletes and places and games is in person, of course, with your own eyes. But in the meantime, we offer here—in pictures and a few words—what we hope is a tempting glimpse and a goad to action. Take a look at these hallowed places and these inspired feats, then go see for yourself. Get out there and bear witness to that once-in-a-generation player or that era-defining team, duck into that legendary stadium or that arena where an athlete once did something so astonishing that we're still talking about it with awe and reverence all these years later. There's time left on the clock, but it's always running.

THE SPORTS

MID-WINTER AT LAMBEAU FIELD

WHERE: *Green Bay, Wisconsin*
WHEN: *December through January*

WHY: IN THE DEAD OF WINTER, EVERY PACKERS HOME game recalls the Ice Bowl, the 1967 championship game against the Cowboys, when the temperature at kickoff was 15 degrees below zero, the wind chill -38 (it would reach -57); neither the refs' whistles nor the marching band's instruments would function in the arctic cold (when referee Norm Schachter blew his whistle on the opening kickoff, it froze to his lips); and field conditions were abominable. Just the way the Packers—and their fans—like it. (Sure enough, the Packers win at home at a rate that approaches 80 percent.)

Green Bay beat Dallas that frigid day, 21–17, on a last-second touchdown for their second-straight NFL title (and fifth in seven years) en route to another win in the AFL–NFL World Championship Game, now known as Super Bowl II. Pro football was by then America's favorite TV sport, the Packers its reigning dynasty, and that Ice Bowl victory on Lambeau's "frozen tundra" left a vivid and permanent impression that this is how football at its best is supposed to look.

Lambeau has since undergone numerous expansions and face-lifts, more than doubling its original capacity to 81,435, while remaining the longest continuously occupied stadium in pro sports. So if, with a gun to your head, you have to choose a single NFL stadium to visit, consider the football history that echoes through the Packers' home, and go ahead and take the Lambeau Leap, even if you wimp out and opt for one of the new heated (or, god forbid, indoor) seats.

Bad weather is good news for the Packers, who often thrive on the frozen tundra, as they did in a 2008 postseason drubbing of Seattle.

TOUR DE FRANCE, MOUNTAIN STAGES

WHERE: *The Alps or Pyrenees*
WHEN: *July*

WHY: THE GRUELING MOUNTAIN STAGES OF THE TOUR ARE the most demanding for the athletes and the most rewarding for spectators, offering steep climbs and breakneck descents by packs of riders amid a scene of extraordinary natural beauty. The race follows a different route each year, but it always alternates between clockwise and counterclockwise circuits of France (with occasional excursions beyond the borders). The eight or nine mountain stages are classified by difficulty on a scale of one to four, plus those so challenging that they're called—we are not kidding—"beyond categories" (*hors categories*).

The modern Tour itself is beyond compare—a traveling road show that moves from town to town in 21 stages over the course of 23 days. It's a far cry from the inaugural event in 1903, an ordeal of six marathon stages, which was reimagined the following year as 19 shorter stages with a large cash prize. That did the trick: interest exploded, and so did the level of competition, followed shortly by all manner of cheating and occasional violence by spectators. Sound familiar?

These days, the Tour is elite in every sense, the very best cycling and an eminently civilized spectator experience. Each of the stages has its charm, from the colorful sight of two hundred tightly packed racers at the start to the ceremonial final laps around the Champs-Élysées. But if you have to choose a single day to watch the world's greatest bicycle race, nothing will top the spectacle of the mountain stages, where, against the backdrop of the Pyrenees or the French Alps, world-class riders press themselves and each other to the very edge of human limits.

The mountain stages demand peak performance from riders and offer spectators a mix of intense competition and peerless beauty.

DUKE VS. CAROLINA AT CAMERON

WHERE: *Cameron Indoor Stadium, Durham, North Carolina*
WHEN: *January–February*

WHY: THERE IS NOTHING QUITE LIKE THE CAMERON crazies, the Duke students who camp out in line in "Krzyzwskiville" to secure seats for home games—the contest with North Carolina being the most coveted of all—and then go berserk in a manner that gives the Blue Devils a home-court advantage that over the past twenty years has helped them win 94 percent of their games at Cameron.

But make no mistake: This is not solely about Duke basketball or the Cameron Crazies, mind-boggling and ear-splitting though they may be (the ambient noise in the arena has been measured at more than 121 decibels, roughly the sound, up close, of a jackhammer on asphalt). First and foremost, it's a showdown between elite programs, and the one most likely to produce a first-rate game; despite year-to-year fluctuations in the quality of all college teams (especially in this lamentable one-and-done era), this matchup is as close as you can get to a sure thing. Duke has won five NCAA championships, gone to twelve Final Fours and churned out a nonstop supply of NBA stars, including eight Rookies of the Year. UNC has been to eighteen Final Fours, won five championships, and has produced some of the greatest NBA players of all time (not the least of them a guy named Jordan).

Then there's the rivalry, which is more like a clash of cultures between two great universities that are only ten miles apart. It's a blood feud that is transformed by the mysterious alchemy of sports into joyous intensity for the players on court and the fans throughout the arena.

In 2016, the Tar Heels faced a typical Duke double whammy: a tough Blue Devils team and an avid—some say diabolical—Cameron crowd.

THE IRON BOWL

WHERE: *Tuscaloosa, Alabama (odd years), Auburn, Alabama (even years)*

WHEN: *Saturday after Thanksgiving*

WHY: THIS IS THE BEATING HEART OF COLLEGE FOOTBALL, an intrastate rivalry as intense and vibrant as you'll find in any state or sport. It's held in a state where Bear Bryant reigned for twenty-five years and led the Crimson Tide to six national championships and thirteen SEC titles against the toughest competition in the land, and a state where Shug Jordan coached the Auburn Tigers for twenty-four years, including seven top-ten seasons and a perfect 10-0 national championship in 1957.

For most of its history, the Iron Bowl was played at a "neutral" site, in Birmingham (less than an hour from Tuscaloosa), and that city's iron-and-steel industry lent the game its name. It's said that Jordan might've been the first to tag it, when he was quoted in 1964, saying, "We've got our bowl game. We have it every year. It's the Iron Bowl in Birmingham."

Like all great rivalries, the Iron Bowl is undergirded by epic feuds, including disputes over officiating and player per diems (don't even ask) that caused a forty-year suspension of the game in the early twentieth century. It's been played every year since 1948, though, and has a double album's worth of greatest hits: the first Iron Bowl on national TV, in 1964, featuring Joe Namath leading 'Bama to a 21–14 win; Auburn's victory in 2010 that led to a BCS national championship—there have been so many big ones. Five consecutive Iron Bowl winners, in fact, went to the BCS championship game from 2010 to 2014. How's that for high-end football rivals locked in eternal battle for bragging rights?

'Bama didn't hit pay dirt here, but led the 2013 classic until Auburn returned a blocked field-goal try for a winning score on the final play.

KENTUCKY DERBY

WHERE: *Churchill Downs, Lexington, Kentucky*
WHEN: *First Saturday in May*

WHY: THE MILE AND A QUARTER OF THE DERBY FOREVER separates one three-year-old colt or filly from the rest of its generation, earning the winner fat breeding fees—and a diverse and active love life—along with a coveted place in the annals of racing. The stakes are as high as they get, which is why the Derby has long been called the most exciting two minutes in sports.

So what exactly is riding on Derby Day (besides twenty jockeys and a couple hundred million in pari-mutuel wagers)? History, for one thing, and like so much else in racing, that history relies deeply on bloodlines. In 1872, Meriweather Lewis Clark (grandson of William Clark, of Lewis and Clark) attended the Epsom Derby and palled around at Longchamp with French Jockey Club swells. Determined on his return to create a similar spectacle for American racing, he cadged land for a track from two uncles named Churchill and organized local fans into the Louisville Jockey Club. And in 1875, voilà! The first Kentucky Derby: 15 horses, 10,000 fans, and a winner: Aristedes.

The race has been run every year since, and, as American spectacle, has traveled light-years beyond anything Clark could've imagined. In 2015, a record 170,513 fans mobbed Churchill Downs on race day. They drank mint juleps—lots of them—and whether they sat on Millionaires' Row or reeled with the shirtless, puking throngs on the infield, they sang "My Old Kentucky Home"and probably teared up a bit (oblivious that the song is about slavery), and then they saw the starting gate slam open and watched the world's best three-year-olds spend the next two minutes deciding which of them would be remembered forever.

With Churchill's twin spires as the backdrop, American Pharoah (running fourth) launched his triumphant Triple Crown campaign.

THE FRENCH OPEN

WHERE: *Stade Roland Garros, Paris, France*
WHEN: *May to June*

WHY: THE SECOND LEG OF THE GRAND SLAM OF TENNIS, played on the distinctive red courts of Roland Garros in downtown Paris, the French Open is undoubtedly the world's premier clay-court tournament. But let's examine the tennis played here as the French would surely examine it: in terms of aesthetics.

Unlike the game played on grass or synthetic hard courts, which magnifies the advantage of big servers, the slow clay of Roland Garros rewards shot-making, court coverage, and endurance. Rallies tend to last longer. The tennis is—how you say?—*plus élégant*, more complex, more subtle.

Pete Sampras, whose booming serve helped carry him to fourteen Grand Slam titles, never won the French. Rafael Nadal, who could stand on the baseline and hit topspin rockets all day and get to anything you hit back at him, has won the French nine times. Serena Williams, whose power supercharges every phase of her game, has won it three times. OK, so style trumps pure power: how French!

Then there's the charm of Roland Garros: the fact that it's easily accessible by the Metro and that the food is better than you'd expect (and you won't have to take out a home-equity loan to pay for it). Furthermore, it's the most intimate of the Grand Slam venues (Court Philippe Chatrier, center stage at the French, now holds a hair under 15,000 spectators).

If all that isn't enough for you, well, what the hell, there's always this: it's springtime, and you're still in Paris.

Stan Wawrinka (in white) beat No. 1 ranked Novak Djokovic in the 2015 final at Roland Garos, then again a year later in the U.S. Open.

FIGURE SKATING, OLYMPIC FINALS

WHERE: *PyeongChang, South Korea; Beijing, China*
WHEN: *February 2018 (South Korea); 2022 (China)*

WHY: THINK BACK TO THE DAYS WHEN FIGURE SKATING championships were among the biggest things in sports and, therefore, on television. We're talking about top-ten all-time Nielsen ratings, right up there with Super Bowls. Interest in skating swelled at every Olympics, where national champions clashed in Battles of the Network Ice Queens. It started with Peggy Fleming (Grenoble, 1968), the first modern media celebrity to cross over from figure skating, and grew with Dorothy Hamill ('76) and Katarina Witt ('84 and '88), through a long era of prosperity. When Tonya Harding and her sidekicks conspired to bust up Nancy Kerrigan's knee in '94, the glamour of skating went tabloid, creating TV ratings unlikely ever to be matched.

Flash-forward twenty years, to a sport that has declined by every conceivable measure—except, of course, the skill and grace of the athletes. So what happened? Many point to the Olympic judging scandal of 2002 and a revised scoring system that alienated fans by making the judging utterly opaque. A steady slump in ratings and ticket sales led to reduced post-Olympic earning power, which led in turn to a revolving door of American skaters.

For all that, the appeal of Olympic skating persists, and the world will surely be watching when the always-powerful Russians and the latest US darlings spin and salchow after the Asian women who have emerged as the sport's dominant force in the twenty-first century. They're not quite the crossover stars of yore, but with a couple billion Chinese fans streaming the Olympics on their iPhones and following their newly crowned ice queens to postgames fame and fortune, that too could change.

Adelina Sotnikova became the latest in a long line of Russian champions when she won gold at the Sochi games in 2014.

START OF THE INDY 500

WHERE: *Indy Motor Speedway, Indianapolis, Indiana*
WHEN: *Memorial Day weekend*

WHY: GENTLEMEN, START YOUR ENGINES. . . . IT'S ONE OF the most famous phrases in all of sport, and it'll be the last thing you hear before the deafening roar of 33 racers firing up their 600–700 horsepower Indy cars and setting out on 200 laps at speeds exceeding 200 miles per hour.

What could be more quintessentially American than a bunch of amped-up guys (until 1977, when Janet Guthrie qualified, it was an exclusively male club) pushing their equally amped-up rides to the max in a death-defying dash for cash (almost $2.5 million to the winner)? The first Indy 500 was run in 1911 and the 100th in 2016, and from the beginning, the formula worked: fast cars, big money. The $25,000 purse in 1911 attracted 40 racers and more than 80,000 spectators.

The Brickyard—a nickname that refers to the material used to resurface the course in 1909—now has a seating capacity of 250,000 and packs another 50,000 on the infield of the 2.5-mile track. Those 33 qualifiers will be stacked in rows of three, and after the gentlemen and ladies start their engines, they will do their best to avoid first-lap mayhem with a rolling start, behind a pace car, just as they did the first hundred times they ran the race. (Well, there was that little incident of mayhem in 1982, when Kevin Cogan, sitting in the middle of the front row, veered sharply as he approached the green flag and took two cars out of the race before it started.) And as always, the 500 will be billed, fittingly, as the Greatest Spectacle in Racing.

When the pace car slides into the pits and the lights turn green, there are only 200 laps and 500 miles to go in America's premier race.

THE GREEN MONSTER

WHERE: *Fenway Park, Boston, Massachusetts*
WHEN: *Early April until late September*

WHY: FENWAY IS THE OLDEST (BUILT IN 1912) AND smallest (37,673 seats) ballpark in the majors, but its fabled left-field wall is the tallest in big-league baseball, standing thirty-seven feet, two inches. Many fans now mention the singing of "Sweet Caroline" as their favorite part of the Fenway experience, but the Green Monster is and forever will be Fenway's signature feature.

The left-field wall, part of Fenway's original construction in 1912, was meant to prevent freeloading fans from viewing the action from Lansdowne Street. Running 231 feet from left to center (all but three feet in fair territory), the original wooden structure was rebuilt with concrete and tin in 1934, at which point Duffy's Cliff, the steep sloping terrace at the foot of the wall (named for Duffy Lewis, the Sox left fielder who mastered the intricacies of playing defense there) was removed and the famous hand-operated scoreboard was installed. Thirteen years later, a paint job transformed what was merely the Wall into the Green Monster.

From the beginning, the wall giveth and the wall taketh away. On the one hand, lazy fly balls that would be easily caught in more spacious parks either ricochet off the Monster for doubles, or worse—at times, much worse (see: Bucky Dent, 1978). On the other hand, hot line drives that would leave the field, if not the ballpark, in many places are reduced to doubles—or less. With Fenway lineups often stacked with right-handed hitters, there is rarely a dull moment. In Boston (as it's often said in another context), every fly ball is an adventure.

The looming monster in left is sometimes friendly to hitters, sometimes not, but it is always a powerful presence.

Monster Numbers

274
Seats installed atop the left-field wall before the 2004 season.

13
Height above the ground, in feet, of the bottom rung of a ladder affixed to the left-field wall, in fair territory, and used to fetch balls from the net atop the Green Monster until the net's removal in 2003.

127
Slots in the hand-operated scoreboard that tracks the ongoing Sox game and out-of-town games.

3
Operators needed to keep the scoreboards current.

13 x 16
Dimensions, in inches, of the 2-pound numbered plates used in scoreboard.

3
Weight, in pounds, of each 16 x 16-inch scoreboard plate that corresponds to the number of the current pitchers in every game.

It takes a three-man crew to hang numbers on the hand-operated scoreboard that tracks the action in Fenway and around the majors.

THE BEAUTIFUL GAME

WHERE: *Estadio Maracanã, Rio de Janeiro, Brazil*
WHEN: *January-April*

WHY: THERE AREN'T ALWAYS 199,854 HYSTERICAL FANS in Maracanã, as there were in 1950, when, needing only a draw in the final to claim the World Cup and widely expected to do so, Brazil lost to Uruguay, 2–1. Uruguay's second goal silenced the enormous crowd and—so the story goes—sent despondent fans leaping to their death from the upper decks. This took its place as the darkest day in Brazil's football history, forever to be known as *Maracanazo*.

The stadium's entire history, in fact, has been a little sketchy, if not downright cursed. Construction began in 1948 and was close enough to completion two years later to host that final, but Maracanã was not officially finished until seventeen years later. Perhaps they rushed it a bit: in 1992, part of the upper deck collapsed, killing three people and injuring at least fifty others. A renovation replaced the original two-tier seating design with a single-tier bowl, reducing the capacity to 78,838 in time for the 2014 World Cup. But redemption for Maracanazo was not yet in the cards: Brazil was eliminated in the semifinals, without playing a single Cup game in the stadium.

A healthy measure of national pride was finally restored with a glorious victory for the home team in the soccer finals at the Rio Olympics. And so Maracanã remains *the* venue in a country long revered as the wellspring of world soccer, hosting games between Brazil's major clubs. Vast armies of fans always turn out to support their beloved Flamengo and Vasco da Gama and Botafogo, and emotions run high and hot in this place. It's Brazil, after all, and there's no soccer here without passion.

A source of pride and a scene of triumph at the Rio Olympics, Maracanã will never shed its link to an epic disappointment.

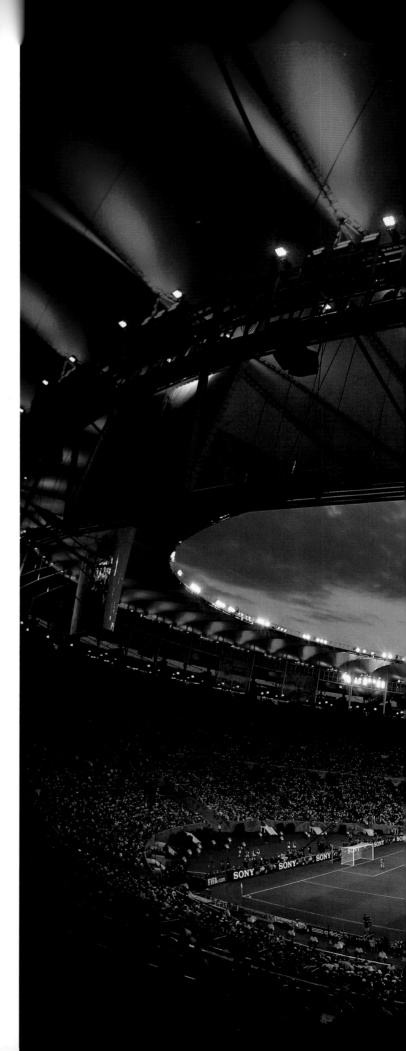

TOUCHDOWN JESUS

WHERE: *Notre Dame Stadium, South Bend, Indiana*
WHEN: *September through December*

WHY: SINCE ITS INSTALLATION IN 1964, THE WORD OF LIFE, a mural by Millard Sheets that adorns the south panel of Notre Dame's Hesburgh Library tower, has reigned over every Fighting Irish home football game, the Savior's arms upraised as if signaling a touchdown. It is the signature feature of one of the fabled venues in American sports.

The mural was clearly visible to spectators and TV cameras for many years, until a mid-nineties expansion (to the current capacity of 80,795) blocked the view from many seats. But by then the image and its nickname had long since taken hold. Notre Dame football, of course, had already earned its place in the sports pantheon and its own religiously devoted following. Since it emerged as a powerhouse team in the Knute Rockne era (1913–1930) and grew into a widely beloved sports institution by way of national radio broadcasts during the thirties and forties, the Fighting Irish enjoyed a far-flung fan base and an unmatched record of sustained excellence: the highest winning percentage of any major-college program (73 percent), 11 national titles, seven Heisman Trophy winners, 50 members of the College Football Hall of Fame, and NFL draftees approaching 500 at last count.

But the numbers tell only part of the story. The rest is left to the mythology of Fighting Irish football. And that will come fully to life when you tour the campus on your way to the game: past the Golden Dome, the Basilica of the Sacred Heart, Fair-Catch Corby, First Down Moses and finally, praise the lord, Touchdown Jesus.

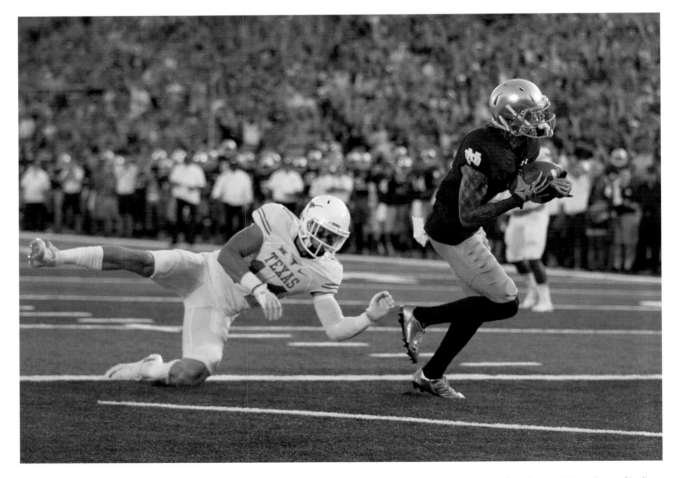

The Irish are blessed by the sacred image that watches over them at all times, but most apparently at home in Notre Dame Stadium.

RUGBY WORLD CUP

WHERE: *Yokohamo, Japan (Finals)*
WHEN: *September 19 to November 2, 2019*

WHY: YOU DON'T HAVE TO KNOW A SCRUM FROM A MAUL to get a huge kick out of rugby, a game of blunt-force physicality that should appeal to the football-loving soul of any American fan. And rugby doesn't get any better than the quadrennial Rugby World Cup (RWC)—a match of muscle and will between national teams for the sport's biggest prize. If you're lucky, they'll throw in a war dance.

This RWC will bring together teams from twenty countries, including the usual powerhouse sides from the Southern Hemisphere that have won seven of the previous eight cups: Australia (three), New Zealand (two), and South Africa (two). Also in the draw will be England, the birthplace of the game and the only other country to win it all, and the host, Japan, whose successful bid to host the tournament—the first Asian country to do so—is a clear sign of the sport's growing reach. Those five teams will join the other qualifiers at a dozen venues around Japan, all leading to the semifinals and final in Yokohama.

As good as the rugby is at this late stage of the proceedings, there are many who believe that it's worth a trip to Japan just to see New Zealand do the Haka, a ceremonial war dance that distills rugby—and, for that matter, all of sport—down to its essence. As they face the opposing team, the All Blacks (as the New Zealand side is known) bellow and grunt as they pantomime the violence they mean to inflict as they subdue and destroy the opponent. All we know is that it's fantastic to watch. And it seems to work for the Kiwis.

The fierce, primal nature of the game was on glorious display when Canada and Italy came to blows in Leeds, England, in the 2015 Cup.

PEBBLE BEACH GOLF LINKS

WHERE: *Pebble Beach, California*
WHEN: *June 13-16, 2019 (U.S. Open); any time (to play)*

WHY: TO HONOR THE CENTENNIAL OF ONE OF THE WORLD'S best-loved layouts, the lords of golf scheduled the 2019 US Open at Pebble Beach. So for the sixth time, the nation's championship will return to this incomparable strip of the California coast between Carmel and Monterey.

It's fairly obvious that of all the hazards players face at Pebble, the greatest is its bedazzling beauty. That was clearly what the designers had in mind when they put all those holes along the coastline and on little peninsulas that jut out into Carmel Bay. The success of their efforts has long been confirmed by universal acclaim, including inclusion on all those lists (often at the top) of the best golf courses in America, best courses in the world, best, you know, anywhere.

And then, as if the place couldn't get by on its looks, it has all that Open history. Recall, for example, just a few of the epic shots on the 17th hole alone: Jack Nicklaus's one-iron off the tee that hit the stick on one bounce and came to rest for a tap-in birdie in '72; or Tom Watson's chip-in bird from the deep Open rough to hold off the charging Nicklaus a decade later. Soon it starts to sound the way it looks: too good to be true. And yet, there it is, open to the public. So join the galleries at the 2019 Open. Or better yet, pony up some of the world's highest greens fees (around $500) and play your own round at Pebble. See for yourself if the place is all it's cracked up to be—the most spectacular golf course in the universe.

The splendor of northern California meets the power of the Pacific on No. 7, a signature hole on this incomparable course.

CARIBBEAN WORLD SERIES

WHERE: *Rotating Sites*
WHEN: *February*

WHY: AS OF 2016, ALMOST 30 PERCENT OF MAJOR LEAGUERS were born outside the United States. At this tournament, which matches the club-level champs of participating nations, you can see budding big leaguers years before they become household names.

If you doubt the level of talent in this series, look closely at the latest MLB figures: out of the 700 players on current 25-man rosters, 230 were born outside the United State, 83 of those in the tiny Dominican Republic. The four other regular participants in the Caribbean Series are also significant contributors to the MLB talent pool: in 2016, Venezuela ranked second with 66; Cuba had 18; Puerto Rico, 13; and Mexico, 9. (Don't be deceived, though; Mexico has won three of the past four series, so there's no dearth of prospective major leaguers there.)

In fact, Mexico became a regular participant only in 1970, but the series goes back to 1949, when major league teams began to drain talent from the Caribbean Leagues by signing black prospects. To forestall any cooling of interest in the winter leagues, a couple of Venezuelan entrepreneurs, Pablo Morales and Oscar Prieto Ortiz, cooked up the Caribbean Series. The original round-robin included Venezuela, Panama, Cuba, and Puerto Rico, a group that lasted until Fidel Castro dissolved pro baseball in Cuba in 1960. The series resumed in 1970 with the current lineup (Cuba rejoined the rotation in 2014) and is now an eight-day tournament, perfectly scheduled for a Caribbean getaway featuring fun, sun, and first-class *beisbol*, just when you're missing it most.

Venezuela hosted a recent series, which rotates sites but always showcases young players from major tributaries to the talent pool.

THE FROZEN FOUR

WHERE: *Excel Center, St. Paul, Minnesota*
WHEN: *April 5-7, 2018*

WHY: WHILE MUCH OF THE NATION IS CAUGHT UP IN MARCH Madness, the puck-heads among us turn their attention to the sixteen Division 1 men's hockey teams in the NCAA tournament that culminates in the Frozen Four. For the first ten years, those climactic games were played in Colorado Springs, but as interest in the college game broadened and intensified, the Frozen Four began to rotate among venues, settling into a series of NHL-scale arenas in the 1970s. And though ESPN has broadcast every game of the tournament for the past decade, the semis and the final have continued to draw swarms of out-of-town fans.

Let us count the reasons why: from the beginning of the tournament, you're sure to get a look at the blue bloods of the sport—the likes of Michigan (nine NCAA titles), North Dakota (eight) and Denver (seven). But there's also a good chance you'll latch on to one of the long shots (Union, Quinnipiac, and Bemidji State come to mind) and get to follow an underdog as it busts through the bracket. It's likely, too, that you'll glimpse a future NHL star or two; in 2016, for instance, there were eighteen players from title-winning NCAA teams in the league. And there's the sheer excitement of the spectacle—the highly partisan fans who travel to big arenas to support their team. Over the past fifteen years, Frozen Four crowds have averaged more than 18,000, which puts them at least on a par with the average NHL attendance during that time. And in 2010, a record 37,592 fans turned up at Ford Field in Detroit to see Boston College crush Wisconsin in the final. But, indoors or out, the Frozen Four is always a hot ticket.

The Frozen Four often seems to pit a dark horse like Quinnipiac (in gold) and a perennial power like BC, as it did in a 2016 semifinal.

THE ROSE BOWL

WHERE: *Pasadena, California*
WHEN: *January 1 (or January 2 if the New Year falls on Sunday)*

WHY: LET'S BE CLEAR: WHEN WE SAY YOU MUST SEE THE Rose Bowl once in your life, what we mean is the postseason football game, though the stadium that shares its name and the parade that precedes it are also part of the appeal. That much you can be sure of, since the game is always played in Rose Bowl Stadium (if you don't count the one played a couple of weeks after Pearl Harbor, which was moved to North Carolina for fear of enemy attack); and it's always on New Year's Day (as long as that doesn't fall on a Sunday—a prohibition that goes back to the 1890s, when it was feared that noise from the Rose Parade would scare the horses hitched outside churches); and except in years when the BCS designates the Rose Bowl as the National Championship Game, as it has twice before (which will make it considerably later).

What else is certain about the Rose Bowl? Well, it will be a showdown of major conferences, pitting the champs of the Pac-12 and the Big Ten (unless one or both of those teams is chosen for the College Football Playoff semifinals, in which case the next-best team in each conference plays). And though it will undoubtedly be first-rate football (the game has featured twenty-nine national champions), the crowd will surely not exceed the record 106,869 who saw number one USC whup number three Ohio State in 1973, because the stadium's capacity has since been reduced by 11,000.

But seriously, folks, the Rose Bowl is an ironclad tradition on New Year's Day (or later, if necessary), because it's the Granddaddy of Them All. That's for sure. And the parade beforehand is a doozy.

It all came up roses for Stanford on a typical winter day in Pasadena, when they dominated Iowa in the 102nd renewal of the grand old game.

OLYMPIC TEAM HANDBALL

WHERE: *Tokyo, Japan*
WHEN: *July 24–August 9, 2020*

WHY: LONGTIME AFICIONADOS SWEAR THAT THE TRUE HEART of the Olympics is found not in the glamour sports whose gold medalists end up on Wheaties boxes but in obscure events, for that's where you can see a life-and-death showdown in a sport you know nothing about, though you might've played something like it once at camp.

Take, for example, team handball. To the unschooled eye, it appears at first to be a landlocked version of water polo, with maybe a little basketball or dodgeball thrown in. Some form of the game seems to have been around forever, but it was codified in the nineteenth century and became popular in northern Europe, which explains why that region is now the hotbed of handball and why the singing, chanting fans you see at Olympic matches all seem to be blondes wearing face paint and speaking Norse languages. Also: why Sweden has won gold medals in four of the last six games.

Those Olympic aficionados are right, and this might be why: When you watch gymnasts or pole-vaulters, it would never occur to you for even a second that you could do what they're doing. But when you watch team handball—or badminton, or archery—you can imagine yourself out on that court, in that game. That's what the sports-marketing geeks call "relatable," and it's as sure a source of spectator thrills as its polar opposite, the awe inspired by an athletic feat that doesn't seem possible for any human—least of all you—to perform, even though you just saw it with your own eyes. But when the nonstop action on a handball court brings you to your feet, you'll feel ready and able to jump into the game. It's right there, within your reach.

The intensity and dedication on display at the Games' less glitzy events might well be the purest expression of the Olympic spirit.

BIG WAVES AT THE EDDIE

WHERE: *Waimea Bay, Oahu, Hawaii*
WHEN: *December-January*

WHY: THE OLDEST OF THE BIG-WAVE SURFING COMPETITIONS, the Eddie is probably still the most prestigious and dangerous. It's the one aptly named for the Hawaiian surf legend Eddie Aikau, the first official lifeguard at Waimea, who rode waves and made rescues that no one else would even try.

Aikau was thirty-one in 1978 when he was crewing on a sea canoe that capsized ten or twelve miles off the coast of Molokai. Crew members clung to the hull, but when no one showed up to rescue them, Eddie paddled off on his surfboard to get help. He was long gone when the Coast Guard finally arrived and fished out the rest of the crew, but he never made it to shore and his body was never found. That story, along with accounts of his fearless big-wave surfing and his lifeguard rescues, make sense of the otherwise puzzling bumper sticker you see around Waimea: EDDIE WOULD GO.

The big-wave event that now honors him is distinguished by its requirement that swells measure at least twenty feet before the event can proceed—which is why it's been held only nine times in the past thirty years. When conditions are up to snuff, though, you can spend hours watching a couple dozen of the world's best surfers take on the man-eating waves.

The big waves win much more often than not, wiping them out, one after another, until someone catches it just right, and survives the drop into the pipe, and disappears under the curl and the crashing spray, and somehow comes out of the whole thing not just alive, but standing.

Even the world's most fearless and skillful surfers face a daunting test when the Eddie gets rolling in the breakers of Waimea Bay.

LITTLE LEAGUE WORLD SERIES

WHERE: *Howard j. Lamade Stadium,
South Williamsport, Pennsylvania*
WHEN: *August*

WHY: THERE'S NOT MUCH THAT'S SMALL THESE DAYS ABOUT the Little League World Series (LLWS). The stadium where the deciding games are played, for instance, has a field about two-thirds the size of those in the pro game, and a seating capacity listed at 45,000 (most of which aren't actually seats, but spots on the berm beyond the outfield fences, where admission is free).

As for the series itself, the charming little event that started in 1947 with eleven teams is now an international goliath, encompassing nine tournaments involving five age groups up to nineteen-year-olds. But all eyes—including the unblinking ESPN cameras that cover the semis and the final—are still on the true Little Leaguers, the eleven-to-thirteen-year-olds. Half of the sixteen teams that make it to the final bracket represent US leagues, while the other half are highly skilled teams from abroad. Before they stopped participating in 1996, in fact, Taiwanese teams had won the LLWS seventeen times, more than anyone else; Japanese teams have been dominant lately, winning four of the last six, until an American team took the title in 2016.

These are the biggest games of their lives for these Little Leaguers, and when you see what outstanding ballplayers they are, how poised and polished under pressure, it's no surprise to learn that scores of LLWS veterans—more than sixty at last count—have gone on to play in the majors. Six players who appeared in the 2004 series alone had made it to the Show by the time they were twenty-five. All to say, these kids are prospects, worth keeping an eye on.

The hours of practice pay off in the polished skills of top teams, but in the series' best moments, these are just kids having fun playing ball.

THE BELMONT STAKES

WHERE: *Belmont Race Course, Elmont, New York*
WHEN: *Fifth Saturday after Derby Day*

WHY: THE BELMONT IS THE OLDEST OF THE TRIPLE CROWN races (the first was in 1867), but more than mere longevity has earned this Grade 1 stakes its nickname: the Test of the Champion. At a mile and a half, it is the longest and most taxing of the Triple Crown races, and it has been the Waterloo of many a Derby and Preakness winner—twenty, to be exact—all extraordinary Thoroughbreds, foiled in their effort to complete one of the rarest trifectas in sports.

You might've thought otherwise if you were around when Seattle Slew (1977) and Affirmed (1978) made Triple Crowns look commonplace. But until then, a quarter century had passed without one, and another thirty-seven years would elapse before American Pharoah repeated the feat in 2015.

It's no wonder that huge crowds turn out for the Belmont, even when there's no Triple Crown on the line. Until attendance was capped at 90,000 in 2015, crowds exceeding 100,000 weren't unusual. Unlike the Derby and the Preakness, the Belmont does not pack spectators on the infield; instead, the sprawling crowds reach all the way down the homestretch of the vast track, where they have to make do with a glimpse of the field turning for home. The ideal place to be, though, is closer to the clubhouse, where you can feel your heart skip as you watch a stretch run that seems endless and see the Belmont winner finally hit the wire. It doesn't take an American Pharoah to make the case that whichever horse is in front at the end of that mile and a half is a champion.

With a triple crown on the line in the 1½-mile marathon, the field left the starting gate in the dust (and shadows) in the 147th Belmont.

Two Out of Three

Twenty Horses have won the Derby and the Preakness, but failed in the Belmont.

Horse	Year / Placed in the Belmont	
Pensive	1944	2nd
Tim Tam	1958	2nd
Carry Back	1961	7th
Northern Dancer	1964	3rd
Kauai King	1966	4th
Foward Pass*	1968	2nd
Majestic Prince	1969	2nd
Canonero ll	1971	4th
Spectactular Bid	1979	3rd
Pleasant Colony	1981	3rd
Alysheba	1987	4th
Sunday Silence	1989	2nd
Silver Charm	1997	2nd
Real Quiet	1998	2nd
Charismatic	1999	3rd
War Emblem	2002	8th
Funny Cide	2003	3rd
Smarty Jones	2004	2nd
Big Brown	2008	DNF
California Chrome	2014	4th

* *Finished first after Stage Door Johnny was DQ'd*

Smarty Jones (9) couldn't hold off Birdstone.

American Pharaoh (5, right) passed the test that so many others could not, completing the Triple Crown in the Belmont.

UCONN WOMEN'S BASKETBALL

WHERE: *Gampel Pavillion, Storrs, Connecticut*
WHEN: *November to February*

WHY: THERE IS ONE SIMPLE AND COMPELLING REASON TO make your way to Storrs for a UConn game: to behold a dynasty. The hard part about discussing the Huskies is finding a worthy basis of comparison. John Wooden's UCLA teams come to mind, of course, and maybe the New York Yankees (27 championships, including 19 in one 36-year stretch). But when you compare records of sustained excellence, some pretty good teams don't hold up against UConn's (Jordan's Bulls), or not yet, anyway (Curry's 73-win Warriors).

UConn has had 10 national championships . . . in this century, 11 overall, including back-to-back perfect seasons. How good have UConn's players been? Twenty were WNBA first-rounders in the league's first twenty years, including five number-one overall picks, Sue Bird, Diana Taurasi, Tina Charles, Maya Moore, and Breanna Stewart. In her time, each prompted the same discussion: "Is she the greatest woman college player ever?" Geno Auriemma coached them all in his 31 seasons (through 2015–2016) and has the highest winning percentage (87.7) of any NCAA basketball coach, men's or women's, who's lasted at least a decade. (Incidentally, if UConn is playing for the NCAA title, men's or women's, don't bet against them: they've never lost a final.)

There have been a few stretches that qualify as down years, if only by UConn standards. But unless the graduation in 2016 of Breanna Stewart, Moriah Jefferson, and Morgan Tuck—the top three WNBA draft picks—triggers a long and unprecedented slump at Gampel, what you'll see there is a killer dynasty.

Stewart was astonishing even by UConn's standards, clinching her fourth straight national title in the 2016 Final against Syracuse.

MOUNT EVEREST BASE CAMP

WHERE: *Nepal (28°0' 26'N 86°51' 34'E)*
WHEN: *March through April, September through October*

WHY: THIS IS THE CLOSEST YOU CAN COME TO CLIMBING Mount Everest without actually climbing Mount Everest. But don't get the wrong idea: it's no stroll in the park (though it will include one, at Nepal's Sagarmatha National Park). First you have to fly to Kathmandu, then take a small plane over the mountains to Lukla. That's where the walking begins, roughly a two-week trek to extreme elevations, led by Sherpas and with frequent stops to acclimate to the altitude. So, we're flying halfway around the world and then walking way uphill until we reach the Everest base camp, and then not attempting to summit the world's highest peak? Isn't that like tailgating at the seventh game of the World Series, then skipping the game and heading home to watch it on your flat screen?

Well, yes and no. You are climbing to an elevation of roughly 18,000 feet through the most spectacular mountain scenery on the planet, and you'll arrive at a place that's within spitting distance of the world's preeminent symbol of challenge and adventure, a 29,029-foot peak. Even there at the base camp, the weather can change suddenly and dramatically, and extraordinary things can happen. The 7.8 earthquake that shook Nepal in April 2015 triggered an avalanche that swept through the camp, killing nineteen people. And yet trekkers and climbers keep coming, as they always have, some 40,000 of them every year, to the foot of the famous Khumbu icefall. That's where mountaineers begin their final ascent to the summit of Everest, because it's there. And you can see it perfectly, because you're here.

At 18,000 feet, might feel like the top of the world, except that Everest itself rises another two miles toward the heavens.

SUNDAY AT THE MASTERS

WHERE: *Augusta National Golf Club, Augusta, Georgia*
WHEN: *April*

WHY: AS DAN JENKINS FAMOUSLY SAID, THE MASTERS doesn't really begin until the back nine on Sunday, and there's no better place to watch that drama unfold than from behind the 12th tee, where you straddle what might be the most famous trio of golf holes in the world, Amen Corner.

Of course, many champions have gone wire-to-wire at Augusta, leading after every round of the tournament. Horton Smith did it in the very first Masters, in 1934, a feat duplicated for the forty-fourth time by Jordan Spieth in 2015. In fact, more than half of all Masters winners have held or shared the lead after three rounds. But all those front-runners hardly put the lie to Jenkins's old saw about Sunday at Augusta.

Even if you take a lead to the 10th hole, you still have to endure the final-round pressure that ratchets up through Amen Corner and beyond, to win the green jacket, the most coveted ugly sports coat in sports.

For a fan, number 12, the heart of Amen Corner, is an ideal vantage point late in the fourth round. With a full-frontal view of the slender green, the beckoning traps, and the swirling winds of that treacherous little par three, you can also glimpse approach shots to the 11th green over your left shoulder and hear the smack of drivers on the 13th tee to your right.

And when the moment of truth arrives, you can make a dash for the 18th hole to see who finally emerges in triumph—and in one piece—from the pressure cooker.

The road to a Masters title runs through Amen Corner, where final-round pressure can turn this tricky par-3 into a little shop of horrors.

ORIOLE PARK AT CAMDEN YARDS

WHERE: *Baltimore, Maryland*
WHEN: *April to September*

WHY: WHEN IT OPENED TO WIDE ACCLAIM IN 1992, Camden Yards kicked off one of the most felicitous trends in modern sports—it was the first of a generation of retro, downtown, baseball-only stadiums that have sprung up throughout the major leagues, changing the architectural face of the game.

In the era Before Camden (BC), the typical modern stadium was a symmetrical, multiuse, large-capacity bowl, like Memorial Stadium, the longtime home of the Orioles and the NFL Colts. When the Colts bolted for Indianapolis in 1984 after failing to secure a new stadium, Baltimore's city fathers, afraid of also losing the O's, quickly approved financing for a new park. The site was the old rail yard near the soon-to-be revitalized Inner Harbor. The design incorporated (instead of demolishing) the red-brick B&O Warehouse, which became Camden Yards' signature feature, and its asymmetrical shape became a hallmark of the modern ballpark.

Widely celebrated as a fan-friendly embodiment of baseball nostalgia, Camden Yards also became a true historical shrine in 1995, during the final as-

sault by Cal Ripken Jr. on Lou Gehrig's record of 2,130 consecutive games, long deemed unbreakable. It's also the only MLB park ever to hold a game with no fans on hand. The O's, flush with young sluggers, are competitive even in the brutally tough AL East, and big crowds turn out for virtually all their games. But after the Baltimore riots in 2015, Camden Yards was closed to the public for an Orioles–White Sox game. The official attendance at the ballpark that day was zero. At almost all other times these days, the place is packed with fans who savor the baseball and the park.

Camden Yards was the prototype of the fan-friendly, baseball-only stadiums that's changed the face of the majors in the past 20 years.

CHEYENNE FRONTIER DAYS

WHERE: *Cheyenne, Wyoming*
WHEN: *July*

WHY: BIG HATS AND BIG CATTLE ARE THE HALLMARKS OF this extravaganza: ten days of high-stakes outdoor professional rodeo, along with what you might call a giant Western exposition, hoedown, and pig-out.

The whole thing started as an old-fashioned roundup—sort of a cowboy job fair—way back in 1897, when Cheyenne was a major crossroads of the booming cattle business. Cowboys came to town to strut their stuff and pick up work, busting broncos and roping steers. Before long, all that morphed into Frontier Days, and when they refer to it as "the Daddy of 'Em All" it's a tip of the ten-gallon hat not just to longevity (the festival is pushing 120, after all), but also to the stature of the rodeo competition.

These days the boom you hear at Frontier Days is not economic but sonic, and it comes from the US Air Force Thunderbirds doing their scheduled fly-overs. Days start with free pancake breakfasts and proceed from there to all manner of diversion, from antique-car parades to Wild West fashion and art shows. And what's become of the old roundup is a big daily dose of rodeo—saddle and bareback bronc riding, steer wrestling, bull riding, and tie-down roping, plus cowgirls and boys slaloming through barrels on fast horses.

Later, the Cheyenne Frontier Days Arena seats 19,000 for country-and-western headliners at the big evening concerts, and no doubt there's plenty of action at those music shows. But for our money there's nothing like watching a cowboy dive off a galloping horse to tackle a runaway steer.

Top-flight pro rodeo by day, music festival by night, Frontier Days is a wide-ranging Western fest that keeps cowboy sports close to its heart.

GOLDEN STATE AT HOME

WHERE: *Oracle Arena, Oakland; Chase Center, San Francisco*
WHEN: *October to June, 2018 (Oracle), 2019 (Chase)*

WHY: HOW DO YOU TURN A PERENNIAL SAD-SACK NBA franchise into a must-see team that fills every venue it plays, at home and on the road? Simple: You buy the Golden State Warriors for $450 million, as the current owners did in 2010. Then you analyze the pro game with a fresh eye and rebuild your roster accordingly, acquiring the players you need to execute your new vision. Easy game, right?

It almost looks that way, at least at this remove. The Warriors were built on the conviction that the three-point shot was a decisive weapon that was grossly underused in the NBA. First they drafted Stephen Curry, a baby-faced assassin who could shoot faster and from farther out than anyone had previously dared. Then, in successive drafts, they added Klay Thompson, another deadly shooter, and Draymond Green, to exploit advantages and minimize vulnerabilities exposed by all that long-rage firepower. Add a few more complementary pieces, and there you have it: a team that won a championship in 2015, then defended it with an unprecedented 73-win season.

Then, when LeBron & Co. brought the Warriors back to earth in the 2016 finals, all they did was sign free-agent Kevin Durant, one of the top five players in the league, and add him to the mix. So now we'll see if Bay Area fans, stalwart through a long era of mediocrity and a few years of renovation, will stay that way when their beloved Dubs move in 2019 from Oracle Arena in Oakland to the Chase Center, their new home across the bay in San Francisco.

Curry's ability to shoot more often and from farther out than anyone ever had made him the keystone in the Warriors' rebuilding plan.

Curry didn't join Durant on the Olympic team (above) but welcomed him to a potent offense that already featured Klay Thompson (right).

Great Seasons, But No Cigar

*Like the 73-win Warriors, these teams had
superb seasons, but no happy ending.*

1995-'96 Detroit Red Wings
Won then-record 62 games, lost to Colorado in Conference Final

2001 Seattle Mariners
Won 116 games, lost to Yankees 4-1 in ALCS

1906 Chicago Cubs
Won 116 of 152 games, lost World Series to White Sox

2007 New England Patriots
After a 16-0 regular season, lost to Giants in Super Bowl

1942 Chicago Bears
Perfect 11-0 season, upset by Redskins in title game

1994 Montreal Expos
Led the majors with 74-40 record when a strike ended the season

1998 Minnesota Vikings
Big Super Bowl favorite after 15-1 season, lost NFC title game to Atlanta

1973 Boston Celtics
Won 68 games (then a record), lost to Knicks in conference final

1991 UNLV Runnin' Rebels
Were 34-0 when they lost to Duke by a basket in NCAA semi-final

1968 Baltimore Colts
Heavily favored NFL champ lost to Jets in Super Bowl III

Future NBA stars Larry Johnson and Grant Hill met in the Final Four.

OHIO STATE VS. MICHIGAN

WHERE: *Ann Arbor, Michigan (odd years),
or Columbus, Ohio (even years)*
WHEN: *Late November*

WHY: IN THE OVERHYPED WORLD OF TWENTY-FIRST-CENTURY sports, this classic contest is notable for its understated nickname alone: the Game—as in, the only one that matters. But there's quite a bit more than that to recommend this storied clash of Big Ten powers.

There are, for instance, the stories. They've been playing the Game since 1897, but it's said that the bitter rivalry goes back even further, to the Toledo War of 1835–1836, a bloodless military standoff over disputed territory along the states' common border. Then there's the sad saga about "Carmen Ohio," the Buckeyes' alma mater, a tearjerker written in 1902 by an OSU freshman on the train home to Columbus after the Wolverines slaughtered the Buckeyes, 86–0.

The pure football tales alone are mythic: There was the Wolverines' 9–3 victory in the Snow Bowl, a 1950 debacle played in a raging blizzard, featuring no offense and forty-five punts, which cost the Buckeyes a Rose Bowl berth—Michigan went to Pasadena—and their coach his job. He was replaced by Woody Hayes, and the Ten-Year War ensued—increasingly bitter battles between his teams and Bo Schembechler's. But the best ever? Maybe the 2006 Game of the Century, both teams 11-0 coming in; No. 1 Ohio State beat No. 2 Michigan, 42–39.

Perhaps this finally says it all: the Big House at Michigan (107,601) and Ohio Stadium (104,944), rank first and third in college football seating, but they're not big enough for the Game; every year since 2001, the reported attendance has exceeded capacity.

Whether it's in Ann Arbor (left) or Columbus, the Game draws a crowd—and inspires passions—that exceed all normal limits.

THE RUNNING OF THE BULLS

WHERE: *Pamplona, Spain*
WHEN: *July 6-14*

WHY: EVERY MORNING AT EIGHT O'CLOCK SHARP DURING the Festival of San Fermín, a small herd of ornery bulls is turned out from the corral of Santa Domingo to stampede through the narrow streets of Pamplona behind a crowd of dashing, lunging people trying to evade or outrun them. This is the famous encierro, the running of the bulls, and about a million people turn out for it every year. Even if you're not normally a livestock fan, this is a show worth seeing.

The running portion of the program (which, if you're eighteen or older, you are free to join) is only about a thousand yards from the corral to the bullring, where the stampede ends and the bulls meet the matadors (and their maker) later that afternoon. The whole dash takes only three or four minutes, so in purely athletic terms, it's a modest proposition. But then there are the imponderables: a couple thousand humans, fleeing the stampede along with you, jostling for position and running for their lives. And don't forget those pesky bulls, with a top speed of 30 to 35 miles per hour (whereas Usain Bolt, for instance, tops out at about 27).

Scores of bipeds are gored, trampled, or otherwise injured every year—there have been fifteen recorded deaths, at last count—so, like other good and brave sports fans around the world, you might decide that spectating is the better part of valor. Temporary fences line the streets of Pamplona's old quarter while the bulls run, so excellent views of the action are available. And if that's not enough to satisfy your craving for blood sport, there's always the corrida, the post-stampede bullfights.

The daily thousand-yard dash through Pamplona's streets demands speed and agility from any runner who hopes to avoid the bulls' fury.

MONUMENT PARK, YANKEE STADIUM

WHERE: *Yankee Stadium, the Bronx, New York*
WHEN: *Old Timer's Day, June*

WHY: IN 1929, A HEADSTONE HONORING MANAGER MILLER Huggins was installed in deep center field at the old stadium, in front of the 461-foot wall; other markers honoring Babe Ruth and Lou Gehrig were added later, leading many kids over the years to believe that the players were buried there. The fence was moved in 44 feet in the mid-seventies, putting the monuments out of play and giving rise to what is now a memorial to beloved Yankees (plus George Steinbrenner).

The House That Ruth Built opened in 1923 and remained the home of the world's most-loved and most-hated team until 2009, when the second-generation stadium made its bow. Many features of the old ballpark were replicated in the new one, including the limestone facade, the signature frieze along the roofline, the short left field porch that makes it baseball's leading home run field, and Monument Park. The whole place breathes baseball history, and you'll never stop hearing it while you're there: 27 World Series championships, 40 pennants, 44 Hall of Famers (a number certain to rise when Mariano Rivera and Derek Jeter are eligible).

Whether you are a Yankee lover or hater—there are few agnostics—a stadium visit is mandatory for anyone who fancies himself a baseball fan. And as long as you're going, why not make it a pinstriped orgy: a guided pregame tour of the stadium (including Monument Park), an Old-Timers' Day game (a nostalgia binge in itself), and a look at the dynasty's latest iteration, a team that, no matter how good, is fated to be measured against a colossus, the immortal Bronx Bombers.

In 2000, long before he was enshrined there—or in Cooperstown—Jeter paid his respects to pinstriped immortals honored in the Bronx.

73

THE NHL WINTER CLASSIC

WHERE: *To be determined*
WHEN: *January*

WHY: THE WINTER CLASSIC IS ONE OF THE LEAGUE'S premier events—the All-Star Game and Stanley Cup are the others—pitting different teams each year in an outdoor celebration of the game's roots in pond hockey. Thanks to its wild popularity, the Classic periodically tests all-time hockey attendance records, like the high-water mark reached at Michigan Stadium in 2014, when 105,491 fans braved the elements to see the Maple Leafs edge the Red Wings 3–2 in a shootout. It's no surprise, then, that every team wants an invitation to the Classic, and every town with a big stadium wants to host it.

At its beginning in 2008, the players donned throwback sweaters for the NHL's celebration of its roots in pond hockey, and the whole show was a huge hit with fans (so were those throwback uniforms, which turned out to sell briskly to fans of all teams, not just those in the Classic). The success was also reflected in the TV ratings—the 2009 renewal, for instance, was the highest-rated NHL game in thirty-three years. In fact, the wild success of the Classic has led the league over the past several years to schedule additional outdoor games during the regular season, and at least a slight backlash was probably inevitable, as columnists and commentators chided the NHL for ruining the game's novelty and diluting its appeal. And sure enough, TV ratings even took a slight hit for the past two Classics, though they still drew more viewers by far than any other regular-season game. So for the time being, at least, the NHL's January outdoor road show is as advertised—a Winter Classic.

In 2001, Wrigley Field joined the venues that have been selected to host the NHL's wildly popular annual tribute to its outdoor roots.

HALFTIME AT FLORIDA A&M

WHERE: *Bragg Memorial Stadium, Tallahassee, Florida*
WHEN: *September to December*

WHY: THE RATTLERS OF FLORIDA A&M UNIVERSITY (FAMU) have won thirteen black college football national championships, so the gridiron action is consistently first-rate at Bragg Stadium. And halftime at every game delivers the unforgettable spectacle of the Marching 100, universally acclaimed as the hottest band anywhere in the world of sports.

There has been a band at Florida A&M since late in the nineteenth century, but the FAMU band as such began when William P. Foster took over as director in 1946. It was Foster who brought real soul to halftime, creating the swaying, high-stepping, double-time dance-march style that made the Marching 100 a dominant brand. During Foster's fifty-two years as the director, the 100 performed at Super Bowls, NBA games, and presidential inaugurations. By 2008, the Marching 100 was 420 strong.

Of course, discussing the Marching 100 without mentioning hazing would be like talking about OJ strictly as a running back. The band was engulfed in scandal and grief after a drum major died from a beating sustained during a hazing ritual in 2011. Ultimately, fifteen band members were convicted or pled guilty in the case, receiving prison sentences as long as six and a half years. An extended period of soul-searching and suspended appearances ensued, while the school confronted the culture of hazing that led to tragedy. But the program resumed in 2013, and one can only hope that the return of the Marching 100 and the joy they inspire will also bring redemption.

The Marching 100 returned to glory after an enforced absence that followed the tragic death of Robert Champion (right) in a 2011 hazing.

THE AUSTRALIAN OPEN

WHERE: *Melbourne Park, Melbourne, Australia*
WHEN: *Final fortnight in January*

WHY: THE FIRST EIGHTY-THREE AUSSIE OPENS WERE played on grass, but with a change of venue in 1988 came the switch to hard courts. Mats Wilander is the only player to have won the Aussie on both grass and hard courts, while Serena Williams and Novak Djokovic have been quite happily confined to the distinctive blue Plexicushion surface on which each has won six singles titles.

As the tournament has grown into one of Australia's most widely viewed sporting events, it has done so while bringing new meaning to the term "hot ticket." The first grand slam on the calendar each year, the Australian falls in the heart of winter in the Northern Hemisphere, which means it's midsummer in Melbourne. That's all well and good, except when a heat wave hits, as it did in 2014, with temperatures reaching 107 to 111 degrees over the course of four days. Nine players retired during first-round action, or just collapsed; at least one reported hallucinating, saying he saw Snoopy before he lost consciousness. Others reported that the soles of their shoes or water bottles began to melt. On the third day, 970 fans were also treated for heat exhaustion.

The good news is that the three primary courts at Melbourne Park have retractable roofs that can be deployed against the sun or rain. And the 2014 heat did nothing to keep the crowds away in the years that followed. It's January, after all, and there are better things to do in Melbourne than worrying about the summer sun—like getting a firsthand look at the new Grand Slam season that kicks off right there.

Serena Williams has been a force in Melbourne, winning the season's first Grand Slam title six times—a feat equaled by Novak Djokovic.

THE DAYTONA 500

WHERE: *Daytona International Speedway, Daytona Beach, Florida*

WHEN: *Last Sunday in February*

WHY: IT'S LIKE PLAYING THE SUPER BOWL ON THE FIRST Sunday of the NFL season, but NASCAR kicks off every year with its most important event, the Great American Race. Miss the opener, the Daytona 500, and you miss the richest (the total purse in 2016 was $18 million) and most prestigious race of all.

With so much cachet and filthy lucre on the line, it stands to reason that since the first Daytona in 1959, the drivers and their teams have always gone flat out to win this one. Whether it was Mario Andretti's first and only win (1967) or Richard Petty's seventh at Daytona ('81); the final lap crash and resulting fisticuffs between Cale Yarborough and the Allison brothers on the first national telecast of the race in '79; or Petty and David Pearson on the final lap in '76, trading paint and the lead before both spun out and only Pearson took the checkered flag; Danica Patrick, the first woman pole-sitter, in '03; or Denny Hamlin edging out Martin Truex Jr. by .01 second, the closest finish ever, in '16, it always makes for quite a show.

And the fans always turn out in force to see it. No official attendance figures are released, but there are 101,000 permanent seats at the speedway, and attendance around the 2.5-mile oval is usually estimated at 250,000. That probably leaves the crowd at Daytona as only the second-biggest at a sporting event in the United States (behind the Indy 500). But then, it's only the first day of the NASCAR season.

The innumerable challenges of NASCAR's annual opener include a mad dash for position after the start and periodic stops in Pit Row.

100-METER OLYMPIC FINAL

WHERE: *Tokyo 2020*
WHEN: *July*

WHY: ATHLETIC CONTESTS DON'T GET ANY PURER THAN THIS: a straight-up footrace, the winner of which is known from sea to shining sea as the world's fastest human. It's a distilled exhibition of power and speed that is the very essence of sports.

From its earliest days, the event captured the public imagination, and fame and glory accrued to Olympic sprint champions, many of whom happened to be Americans. But whatever their nationality, Olympic sprinters gained instant mythic status, from Archie Hahn ("the Milwaukee Meteor," 1904) to Harold Abrahams (the Brit whose quest for the gold in 1924 became *Chariots of Fire*); from Jesse Owens (Berlin, 1936, with Hitler watching) and Wilma Rudolph (Rome, 1960, blazing the trail for generations of dominant African American women sprinters) to Usain Bolt, whose supremacy at three straight Olympics (gold medals in the 100, the 200, and the 4×100 relay) confirmed Jamaica as the sprint capital of the modern world.

True, the Olympic 100s have also had their share of infamy, the taint of steroids reaching from Ben Johnson (1988) through Marion Jones (2000) and up to the wholesale barring of the Russian team from the 2016 Rio games.

But even as reports of drug use inspire new skepticism—and vigilance—throughout sports, the Olympic 100-meter finals have retained their luster and their ability to thrill. The races take less than ten seconds, from blocks to wire, but you have never seen humans run like that before, and never will again.

Usain Bolt's victory in the 100 and the other sprints at the Rio Games only confirmed his status as the greatest of all time.

SPRING TRAINING

WHERE: *Florida and Arizona*
WHEN: *Mid-February through March*

WHY: FOURTEEN DAYS TILL PITCHERS AND CATCHERS. Thirteen days.... Twelve.... You often hear these words pass between baseball fans during the last, brutal weeks of January, like some kind of code or incantation. But it's only the countdown to the launch of another season. For hardcore fans and fantasy-league scouts, spring training has always been the light at the end of winter's tunnel. It's all about seeing the stars of the game up close in charming little ballparks and glimpsing young up-and-comers trying to crack the roster. It's big-league baseball on a human scale.

The ritual of an organized preseason began in the late nineteenth century, when Albert Spalding, the owner of the Chicago White Stockings, had the bright idea to take his team south to Hot Springs, Arkansas, to prepare players for the campaign ahead. The notion caught on and spread—to other teams and other sites—and by the 1920s, the Grapefruit League was in full swing. Bill Veeck took his Indians to train in Arizona in the late 1940s, and soon there was a Cactus League as well.

Fans soon caught on to the pleasures of spring training and made annual pilgrimages, but its popularity exploded only over the past twenty-five years. That made tickets and hotel rooms are a little harder to come by, but it also led to eight new stadiums in Arizona and five in Florida since the mid-1990s. Now that MLB teams are split about equally, east and west, the only tough question is: Cactus or Grapefruit? Either way, it's hard to go wrong when you're sitting in the sun, watching baseball in February.

Fans and coaching staffs get a close look at the talent, be it the Nationals hurlers (left) or the Mets' Curtis Granderson.

CRICKET WORLD CUP FINALS

WHERE: *Lord's Cricket Ground, London, England (2019)*
WHEN: *March through July (depending on venue)*

WHY: THE ULTIMATE SHOWDOWN IN ONE DAY INTERNATIONAL cricket attracts teams from around the globe—in particular, those parts of the globe in or near the erstwhile British Empire. The likes of Sri Lanka and the West Indies now mount spirited and often successful challenges to the traditional powerhouse teams from Great Britain, South Africa, India, Pakistan, and Australia.

Before your American eyes glaze over at the mere mention of cricket, let's be clear that this is not the variety of the game that can go on for days at a time (with appropriate breaks for tea, of course), played for at least 150 years by English gentlemen in white suits. This is the more compact and intense brand of one-day cricket popularized in England in the 1960s, which spread internationally within a decade. It coalesced into the International Cricket Council World Cup tournament in 1975 and has been played every four years since. The tournament now consists of two round-robins of seven teams that have earned entrance through qualifying play; those that survive move to knockout rounds, the quarters and semis, and the championship final.

Alongside this evolutionary development has come radical change: the switch from white to colorful uniforms, to night as well as daytime games, and to the $1.1 billion TV deal for the 2011 and 2015 cups. The last two telecasts attracted some 2.2 billion viewers in 200 countries. So when you start booking flights to London and making plans to check this one off your bucket list, consider that the live gate for cup matches in 2015 was 670,000. You might want to start queuing up now for that final.

The Cup features the brand of cricket that limits matches to a single day and allows colorful uniforms in place of the traditional whites.

HINKLE FIELDHOUSE

WHERE: *Butler University, Indianapolis, Indiana*
WHEN: *March*

WHY: IN A STATE THAT TAKES ITS HOOPS SERIOUSLY, IT IS no small deal for a building to be called Indiana's basketball cathedral. But walk through Hinkle's old-fashioned gymnasium doors and see the arching beams and girders converging above the gleaming hardwood floor, the windows that aren't stained glass but might as well be, and you will know there's something sacred here.

When Hinkle opened in 1928, it was the biggest basketball arena in the country, seating 15,000—far too big, it would seem, for tiny Butler University. The key to Hinkle's funding and its future was a contract to host the culmination of Indiana's basketball tournament, a free-for-all in which, until 1997, the largest and smallest high schools converged in pursuit of a single exalted state title. This is where, in 1954, tiny Milan beat much larger Muncie High to crown its miracle season—a quest that would be the basis for the 1986 classic *Hoosiers*. That film put Hinkle Fieldhouse, where the movie's climactic game was filmed, on the radar of fans everywhere

Sadly, there's no high school hoops at Hinkle anymore—the state tournament (a.k.a. Hoosier Hysteria) is now broken into divisions and played elsewhere—but Butler basketball, after consecutive trips to the NCAA final in 2010 and 2011, has an aura of its own. And so, a newly renovated Hinkle Fieldhouse—with capacity reduced to 9,100 but comfort and cosmetics greatly enhanced—stands as not simply a local shrine but as a US National Historic Monument, to be treasured for its role in the development of basketball in Indiana—which is to say: of basketball, period.

Hoosiers put Hinkle and Indiana's high school tournament on the worldwide radar, and Butler's D-1 success has helped keep it there.

GYMNASTICS
OLYMPIC FINALS

WHERE: *Olympic Gymnastics, Olympic Finals*
WHEN: *July 2020*

WHY: THE GYMNASTICS FINALS ARE THE SUMMER OLYMPIC events where young women become global stars and, on occasion, portraits on Wheaties boxes: Olga Korbut, Nadia Comaneci, Mary Lou Retton, Shannon Miller, Gabby Douglas, Simone Biles—tiny, powerful athletes who captivate TV viewers by the tens of millions, flying through the air and doing impossible things on mats and bars and beams.

Women's gymnastics didn't join the Olympic party until 1928, but you'd have to say the modern era began when Nadia Comaneci, the fourteen-year-old Romanian pixie, "stole the show" (as *Sports Illustrated* said on its cover) at the 1976 games, rocketing to stardom by scoring the first-ever perfect 10s. You can draw the line straight from Comaneci (and her coach, Bela Karolyi, who would defect to the West) to Retton in LA in '84, the first US all-around gold medalist, and onward to the aforementioned American stars. Along the way, women's gymnastics became one of the leading TV draws of the summer games, making them unimaginably valuable—which is why US media rights to the games through 2020 went to NBC in 2011 for $4.38 billion, a deal topped in 2014 when NBC went all-in from 2022 to 2032 games for another $7.75 billion.

All the while, the appeal of the event has never flagged. And thanks to the structure of the competition—team and individual events in each of the four disciplines (bar, beam, vault, and floor exercise)—there are ample opportunities at every Olympics to see a gold medal final, as they say, up close and personal.

After Rio, Biles was the consensus pick as history's greatest gymnast, able, it seemed, to walk on water or upside down on the beam.

Rio 2016

Leading U.S. Medal Winners

The roster of America's repeat gymnastics medalists is a long one. This is just the top of the list.

Years	Gold	Silver	Bronze	Total
SHANNON MILLER 1992, '96	2	2	3	7
ALY RAISMAN 2012, '16	3	2	1	6
SIMONE BILES 2016	4	0	1	5
NASTIA LIUKIN 2008	1	3	1	5
MARY LOU RETTON 1984	1	2	2	5
DOMINIQUE DAWES 1992, '96, 2000	1	0	3	4
SHAWN JOHNSON 2008	1	3	0	4

The performance by Raisman (right) in 2016 propelled her up the list of leading US medalists that includes MIller (above) and Retton (top).

NCAA LACROSSE FINAL FOUR

WHERE: *Gillette Stadium, Foxboro, Massachusetts*
WHEN: *Memorial Day Weekend, 2018*

WHY: THE NCAA DIVISION 1 COLLEGE LACROSSE FINAL FOUR is now held every year in an NFL stadium. That should tell you something about the evolution of a sport that wasn't deemed worthy of a postseason tournament at all until 1971.

According to the NCAA, participation in men's and women's lacrosse grew faster than in any other college sport between 2000 and 2014—up 109 percent for women and 95 percent for men. Apparently, all those kids we saw before the millennium, running around, spinning and twirling sticks, and practicing with youth teams and in backyard nets, have grown up and are playing college lacrosse.

Many of those kids, if they were good, played for schools in the mid-Atlantic and northeastern states, where the toughest competition in the college game has long been concentrated. Only eight teams have won multiple NCAA titles, and all are from that region: Syracuse (10), Johns Hopkins (9), Princeton (6), North Carolina (5), Virginia (5), Duke and Cornell (3), and Maryland (2). No team outside the Eastern time zone won the title until Denver did it in 2015. But that, too, is likely to change, as kids reach college age in places like California and Oregon, where youth and NCAA participation is booming.

Which is not to say that lacrosse is worth watching only now that it's big enough to put its college final in venues built for pro football. As the game is reaching new heights as a spectator sport, it's time to see firsthand, and at its highest college level, what all the excitement is about.

A 2007 semi-final between Cornell and Duke featured two of the eight perennial powers that have won multiple NCAA titles.

ENGLAND VS. THE WORLD

WHERE: *Wembley Stadium, London, England*
WHEN: *September through November*

WHY: ENGLAND AND WEMBLEY ARE FOREVER LINKED, the world's oldest national team and its home field, the site of its greatest glory—that victory over Germany in the 1966 World Cup final. It's the only cup (or its biennial alternate, the European Championship) that the Three Lions have ever won.

Through the ups and downs of international play in the last century—mostly downs—the English home ground was Wembley, first the original stadium, which opened in 1923, then its 2007 replacement, with its 90,000 seats and retractable roof, its signature 440-foot arch, and all the modern comforts (including 2,618 toilets, by some accounts a world record for stadiums). Like the staggering cost overruns and delays during its five years of construction, everything about Wembley has been endlessly debated, including the quality of its pitch, which has been blamed for some of England's failures and so replaced or relaid at least a dozen times. If the grass gets that kind of scrutiny, one can only imagine what it's like to be Roy Hodgson, whose job since 2012 as the national team's manager has been likened in importance to that of the prime minister. Or think of poor Wayne Rooney, who at thirty-one was clearly on the downside of an illustrious career, but who was still the captain and central scoring threat, yet took flak for interfering with the development of promising young stars like Dele Alli and Eric Dier. It seems they just can't win—and yet we can't take our eyes off them, even for a second. Such is life for England and for Wembley, the home pitch, for good or ill, in a nation obsessed with soccer.

In the perpetual debate over its international flops, England's star (Rooney) and its home pitch (Wembley) are targets of endless quibbles.

THE BREW CREW AND BRATS

WHERE: *Miller Park, Milwaukee, Wisconsin*
WHEN: *April to September*

WHY: THEY LOVE THEIR BASEBALL AND THEIR BRATWURST in Milwaukee. And that combination, delivered in the environs of Miller Park and washed down with plenty of the namesake beverage, makes for an unparalleled gastro-athletic experience.

It all starts with the baseball, of course. Milwaukee's first team, the Braves, resided there for thirteen seasons before fleeing for Atlanta in 1966. Part-owner Bud Selig, who had tried to block the move, came to the rescue when he bought the expansion Seattle Pilots out of bankruptcy after one failed season and moved them to Milwaukee as the Brewers in 1970. It took a while for the once-spurned NL fans to embrace their new AL team, but the Brewers hit their stride and the fans returned to baseball; a pennant in 1982 didn't hurt, and neither did Miller Park, which replaced forty-eight-year-old County Stadium in 2001. Maybe there'd never be another Hank Aaron, but the Brewers have produced three MVPs (Rollie Fingers, Robin Yount, and Ryan Braun), while two stalwarts, Paul Molitor and Yount, have made it to Cooperstown. And the fans have stuck by the Brew Crew.

That is abundantly clear the minute you show up for pregame warm-ups—outside the stadium, that is, in the parking lot. What you'll find there is by far the best tailgating scene in baseball. Miller Park's enormous lot has room for more than 12,000 cars, and plenty of space to spare for all those charcoal grills. There's baseball on tap, but first you get the brats and the beer that made Milwaukee famous. It's a Brewers game, after all.

Milwaukee's 2011 ALDS victory (right) was a passing success, but Miller Park and its tailgating tradition always rate among baseball's best.

THE 24 HOURS OF LE MANS

WHERE: *Circuit de la Sarthe, Le Mans, France*
WHEN: *June*

WHY: SINCE 1923, LE MANS HAS BEEN THE BE-ALL AND end-all of Grand Prix endurance sports car racing, a grueling test of equipment and driving skills. The final leg of the so-called Triple Crown of Motorsports (the Indy 500 and the Monaco Grand Prix are the others), Le Mans is the one that puts the biggest premium on fuel efficiency and reliability.

Two general classes of cars run at Le Mans—highly designed prototypes and grand-touring cars (racing machines that resemble street-legal sports cars). These separate but overlapping challenges make Le Mans a crucible of engineering, the results of which tend to trickle down to consumers. In the 2016 race, for instance, new technology got a stern performance test in a Toyota hybrid that was locked in a tight race with a Porsche and looked like the winner until it finally broke down after 23 hours and 57 minutes.

What meets the eye of the spectator at Le Mans, though, is very basic: drivers of fast cars, maintaining high speeds for longer than seems humanly possible. Since duration, not distance, dictates the start and finish of the race, the winner is the car that completes the most laps in 24 hours. The circuit is now 8.4 miles around, and the fastest cars top out at over 200 miles per hour. In the time allotted, the winners these days cover more than 3,000 miles. Just think of it as roughly six Indy 500s, or 18 Monaco Grands Prix, or maybe a New York-to-LA road trip at 200 miles per hour, with enough time left over for a little swing up the switchbacks of the Coast Highway to San Francisco.

The 2013 Le Mans was the 90th renewal of motorsports' ultimate test of engineering and endurance driving.

HERSHEY ARENA

WHERE: *Hershey, Pennsylvania*
WHEN: *November to March*

WHY: GENERATIONS OF BASKETBALL FANS HAVE CLAIMED they were in the building in 1962 when Wilt Chamberlain scored one hundred points. Untold thousands have regaled fellow fans with memories of that golden night in Madison Square Garden when Wilt the Stilt did the impossible. In fact, the game wasn't played in the Garden, but in Hershey Arena, a drafty hockey arena they still call it the Old Barn; and there were only 4,124 souls on hand for the record-smashing scoring binge that night, a 169–147 win by Wilt's Philadelphia Warriors over the New York Knicks.

Because no member of the New York press was there to cover or photograph the game—the Knicks were a last-place team in a struggling league that still scheduled the odd game in places like Hershey—and no film or video record exists, the mythic dimensions of the game (and the number of "witnesses") have only grown. But among the verifiable facts are these: Wilt converted 36 of 63 field goal attempts that night and, though he was a notoriously weak free throw shooter, went 28 of 32 from the line. It was a freakish peak to a season in which Chamberlain averaged 50.4 points and 25.7 rebounds per game (and failed to win the MVP).

The arena is still hosting hockey games, as always, but it's best remembered for a single NBA game played more than fifty years ago. You can see the current college tenants, Lebanon Valley and Shippensburg, play on their home ice there (and while you're in the neighborhood, you can see the AHL stalwart Hershey Bears, the home team at Hershey for sixty-six years, at their new arena nearby). And unlike so many who only imagined it, you can truthfully say you were really in the building where (if not when) Wilt the Stilt scored his hundred.

Wilt Rules

Wilt Chamberlain accounted for 23 of the 33 highest-scoring games in NBA history, including four games in the seventies and 19 in the sixties. Here are the other high scorers and their biggest games.

Points	Player	Team	Year
81	KOBE BRYANT	*Lakers*	2006
73	DAVID THOMPSON	*Nuggets*	1978
71	ELGIN BAYLOR	*Lakers*	1960
71	DAVID ROBINSON	*Spurs*	1994
69	MICHAEL JORDAN	*Bulls*	1990
68	PETE MARAVICH	*Jazz*	1977
65	KOBE BRYANT	*Lakers*	2007
64	ELGIN BAYLOR	*Lakers*	1959
64	RICK BARRY	*Warriors*	1974
63	JOE FULKS	*Warriors*	1949
63	JERRY WEST	*Lakers*	1962
63	GEORGE GERVIN	*Spurs*	1978

A 73-point game by the spectacular Thompson was hardly a fluke.

The iconic image from Hershey's epic: Wilt beams at his total, hastily scrawled on a sheet of paper by legendary stat man Harvey Pollack.

THE CUBS AT WRIGLEY

WHERE: *1060 West Addison St., Chicago, Illinois*
WHEN: *April to September*

WHY: IT MIGHT BE ONLY THE SECOND-OLDEST AND second-smallest major-league stadium, but many believe Wrigley's charms surpass those of any ballpark anywhere.

There are many ways in which it's unique. Most obvious is the ivy that covers the outfield wall, purchased and planted by then-GM Bill Veeck in 1937 and still liable to gobble up fly balls or even outfielders. Wrigley was the first place where fans could keep foul balls hit out of play and the first where homers by visiting teams were routinely thrown back onto the field with extreme (though ironic) prejudice. It is a place where the center-field flagpole flies a white pennant after Cubs' wins and a blue one after losses. And it's a place where you can join 40,000 or so out-of-tune revelers—and the ghost of Harry Caray—singing "Take Me Out to the Ball Game" during the seventh-inning stretch.

It is also the only park in the majors where the wind can have such a powerful and contrary impact (sometimes in the space of a single game), at times blowing in off Lake Michigan, knocking down every hard-hit ball, and at others blowing out, turning every warning-track pop into a homer. And speaking of weather, there was a drought at Wrigley—the one that, until 2016, left the Cubs without a World Series appearance since 1945 (or a championship since 1908). Despite their trials and tribulations—or perhaps because of them—Cubs fans have a highly developed sense of humor and a love of baseball that stands up to any ill winds that might (and probably will) blow through the Friendly Confines. It's a singular pleasure to sit among them.

Wrigley's ivy, the most obvious of its many charms, has engulfed many a fly ball and more than a few Cubs, including Moises Alou.

OLYMPIC SKI JUMPING

WHERE: *PyeongChang, South Korea; Bejing, China*
WHEN: *February 2018 (South Korea); 2022 (China)*

WHY: THIS CRAZY COUSIN OF SKIING WAS INVENTED IN Norway and evolved there from a kind of daredevil demonstration sport—think nineteenth-century X Games—into formal competition. Norwegian emigrants brought it to the US, where the first ski jump contest, in 1887, was won by—who else—a Norwegian. The Americans have been losing to various Scandinavians ever since, while Norway has won more Olympic ski jumping medals than any other country.

The all-time greatest individual performance by an Olympic ski jumper, though, was not by a Norwegian, but a Finn, Matti Nykanen, who in Calgary in 1988 won both the 70- and 90-meter individual events, then took a third gold medal by leading Finland to victory in the team competition.

Competing (barely) against Nykanen was a grinning Englishman with Coke-bottle glasses named Michael Edwards, better known, then and now, as Eddie the Eagle. A 24-year-old plasterer with an Olympic dream, Edwards scrapped his way through the qualifying process and became a worldwide celebrity in an event in which skiers rocket down a hill at about 60 miles per hour and launch themselves into the air, landing some 400 feet away, mostly on their feet. Was Eddie the Eagle an inspirational underdog or a hapless clown, making a mockery of this dangerous sport? Only this much can be said for certain: Matti Nykanen is remembered only by Finns and a few hardcore ski jump fans, whereas a feature film was released in 2016 recounting the trials and triumphs of Eddie the Eagle. One way or another, Olympic ski jumping will give you something to remember.

At the Sochi Games, ski jumpers took flight in events on the 70-meter and 90-meter hills, and in the Nordic Combined (right).

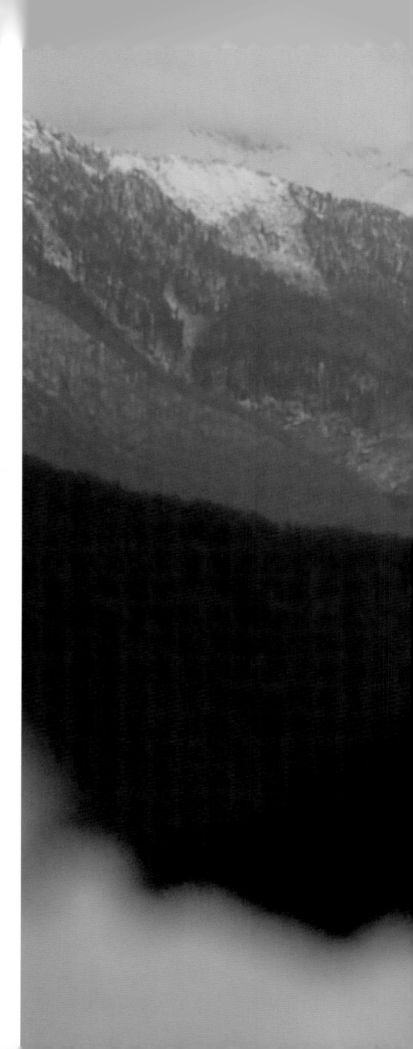

RED RIVER SHOOTOUT

WHERE: *Cotton Bowl, Dallas, Texas*
WHEN: *October*

WHY: TRADITIONALLY HELD DURING THE SECOND WEEK of the Texas State Fair, this fabled rivalry game between Texas and Oklahoma, universities from adjacent states where football is king—was first played in 1900, even before the teams were known as the Longhorns and the Sooners.

Before we size up the game on its football merits and book our tickets to Dallas, consider this: after 100 years, the new sponsors of the Red River Shootout changed its name first to the SBC Red River Rivalry and later to the AT&T Red River Showdown, apparently in an effort to avoid the appearance of condoning gun violence. But let's be real: as long as Texas and Oklahoma are both open-carry states, expunging "shootout" from this game's name is like firing blanks—noisy but pointless.

Aside from that corporate patina, though, what does a 100-year-old football game look like, historically speaking? Well, for one thing, when they started playing this thing, Oklahoma wasn't even a state (the Territories joined the Union in 1907). For another, though each team has had a period of sustained domination—Oklahoma during the fifties, Texas during the forties and sixties—neither side is conceding anything: Texas has won 61 times, Oklahoma 41 (with five ties). The game has matched top-twenty teams 37 times since polling began in 1936, and top-ten teams 14 times. Any year might be a repeat of the famous 1963 game, when number No.2 Texas beat then-No.1 Oklahoma, snatching the top ranking and its first national championship. Now *that* is a shootout.

The Cotton Bowl has been spruced up and expanded since the 2006 Shootout (left), largely to ensure that the game remains in Dallas.

U.S. OPEN, OUTER COURTS

WHERE: *USTA National Tennis Center, Flushing, New York*
WHEN: *September*

WHY: WHEN YOU MAKE YOUR PILGRIMAGE TO THE open, you'll surely want to buy a seat at Arthur Ashe or the next iteration of the old Louis Armstrong Stadium to watch the world's top players while sipping ransom-priced cocktails from souvenir tumblers. There's much to be said for every bit of that experience, but for a taste of tennis like you'll get nowhere else, you have to stroll the outer courts, where you can grab a bleacher seat and see tomorrow's superstars today, up close, like watching Serena or Rafa hitting at your local public courts.

Yes, the Open is thick with tradition, as one would expect of a national championship played continuously since 1881. Well known to tennis aficionados but often overlooked by first-time visitors is the passion play you can witness on the thirteen "field courts," just a short walk from the premium-priced venues. What you find here is not a distant view of jaded draw-fillers, simply going through the motions. Quite the opposite, in fact: the players are among the top one hundred in the world, and you are close enough to hear every breath they take. The desire and raw emotion can be palpable, as young players square off, scrapping to advance a round or two, to prove they belong. And often, as if on cue, the courtside bleachers suddenly fill with fans involved in the match as intensely and vocally as the players.

Sure, you'll remember the stars you saw in the big arena, but if you keep your eyes peeled, you might catch lightning in a bottle at one of these outer-court classics and get a close-up glimpse of the tennis future.

Recent upgrades in Flushing included a renovation of the field courts, which made one of the Open's most appealing features even better.

THE EPSOM DERBY

WHERE: *Epsom Downs, Surrey, England*
WHEN: *First Saturday in June*

WHY: THE RICHEST (£1.5 MILLION IN 2017) AND MOST prestigious of Britain's Triple Crown races, the Derby, like its namesakes at tracks around the world, inspires keen interest that reaches far beyond the racing public and draws an enormous TV audience across the United Kingdom, where, like its offspring in Kentucky, it is the one horse race everyone watches.

Its proper name is the Derby Stakes at Epsom. Legend has it that the two original sponsors of the race—Sir Charles Bunbury and the twelfth Earl of Derby—flipped a coin to determine whose name it would bear. Had it gone the other way, we in the colonies might all be atwitter each May about a race called the Kentucky Bunbury. Lord Bunbury had this consolation, at least: he owned Diomed, the winner of that first Derby.

The race has been run 237 times, every year except those at the height of the two world wars. Almost from the beginning, the Derby (the Brits pronounce it DAR-bee) was—and remains to this day—the centerpiece of a festival featuring all manner of entertainment, attracting large, diverse crowds to Epsom. Originally raced at one mile, the Derby soon became a sterner test for three-year-olds, a mile and a half (plus ten yards), on the turf (or, as we Yanks would call it, the grass). Whatever you call it and however you pronounce it, the Derby is a showcase for the best-bred racehorses in the world (to say nothing of the humans), a venerable sporting event, and a spectacle that is simply without peer.

The Queen was on hand in 2015, as she usually is on Derby day, to see Golden Horn win the 236th running of the England's biggest race.

THE CANUCKS AT HOME

WHERE: *Rogers Arena, Vancouver, Canada*
WHEN: *October to April*

WHY: ANY REASON IS A GOOD ENOUGH REASON TO visit Vancouver, a city that often tops those rankings of the best places in the world to live. Now add this morsel to all the city's other virtues: at the scene of the 2010 Olympics and Canada's favorite memory of those games—a victory over the United States in the gold medal final of men's hockey, in the building then known as the Vancouver Olympic Arena—you can now join the indefatigable fans who turn out to support their the Canucks in their quest for an NHL championship.

You've got to love a hockey team whose name is either a mild epithet for Canadians (in American slang, that is) or an homage to Johnny Canuck, a Bunyonesque logger, hockey player, and Canadian folk hero up in the Great North. And what better home for such a humble team than an arena that's always been affectionately nicknamed the Garage.

Since their entry into the NHL as an expansion team in 1970, the Canucks have had a record of mediocrity punctuated by occasional near misses in the ongoing quest for an NHL championship. The last two close calls were terrible teases for Canucks fans, coming as they did in seventh-game losses in the Stanley Cup Finals (first to the New York Rangers in 1994 and then to the Boston Bruins in 2011).

Both of those losses, by the way, were followed promptly by prolonged rioting in the streets of Vancouver, precisely the sort of thing that residents of this urban Eden still believe should happen only in large American cities.

Among the Vancouver's many wonders is the unflagging support the Canucks have enjoyed from fans through almost 50 years of Cup futility.

THE THUNDER IN OKC

WHERE: *Chesapeake Energy Arena, Oklahoma City, Oklahoma*
WHEN: *November to May*

WHY: THE THUNDERING HERD OF OKLAHOMA CITY FANS have earned their team's arena a reputation as the loudest house in the NBA. Earplugs are beside the point, because when the fans in OKC show their Thunder a little love, you don't just hear it, you feel it. And it's not just noise. It's devotion.

There are many reasons for this special relationship, which began even before the team was especially good: the Thunder is the only pro game in town, so the fans' passion doesn't have to be shared, particularly once football season ends. And though the franchise seems as native to OKC as the owner, Clay Bennett, it was only 2008 when the team was adopted—some say snatched—from Seattle and moved to Oklahoma, where a loving fan base and a spiffed-up new arena were waiting.

The Thunder were terrible at first, a shambles of a franchise, but had an appealing Rookie of the Year in Kevin Durant, a star whose palpable decency suited his new home to a T. They also had a brilliant young GM in Sam Presti, who, starting with Russell Westbrook, built a team around KD that had character equal to its talent. Presto! It all happened fast: a division title in 2011, then a conference championship and perennial postseason play. It was as if the SuperSonics never existed, as if the Thunder were a natural-born child of OKC. It was the perfect rebuilding and rebranding of an NBA team—a job that will obviously need redoing now that Durant has taken his talents to Golden State. But it's hard to believe that the fans of OKC will lose faith in the Thunder. After all, they've seen their team transformed before.

The Thunder and their vocal supporters in OKC will have to lean hard on Westbrook since his former costar set out for points west.

OLYMPIC SNOWBOARDING

WHERE: *PyeongChang, South Korea; Beijing, China*
WHEN: *February 2018 (South Korea); 2022 (China)*

WHY: ONE OF THE REVELATIONS OF THE SOCHI GAMES WAS the ascension of snowboarding from the Olympic fringe to center stage. The sport's various disciplines—parallel slalom and slopestyle joined the halfpipe and snowboard cross among the ten boarding events in 2014—received tons of airtime and generated intense online action, all of which added up to big numbers in the coveted 18-to-24-year-old demographic. Snowboarding came of age as a media phenomenon—which is to say, a spectator sport—by demonstrating its appeal to youth.

That popularity had long been apparent on slopes across the United States, where, for thirty years or more, growing numbers of boarders crossed paths (and often sabers) with traditional skiers. A sport born and popularized in America was already sharply on the rise in 1985, when the James Bond movie *A View to Kill* featured an action-packed snowboard chase (with a champion boarder as the primary stunt double for Roger Moore) that helped supercharge the sport internationally. The debut of Olympic boarding followed in 1998, at Nagano, without even a previous appearance as a demonstration sport at the games.

The rest is history—or would be, except that boarders are still aiming for even more of the Olympic action, pushing slopestyle and big air for full-scale inclusion. And we'll know before long if a sport with cultural roots in skateboarding and surfing and strong family ties to the X Games can cuddle up with old-timey snow sports and get comfy in its place as the new Olympic darling.

Pierre Vautier of France (second from right) took the gold in Sochi in the snowboard cross, which was a huge hit with Olympic viewers.

PRESTWICK GOLF CLUB

WHERE: *Prestwick, South Ayrshire, Scotland*
WHEN: *May to September*

WHY: IT'S HARD TO BELIEVE, BUT THE BIRTHPLACE OF THE Open Championship in the home of golf is only about thirty miles from Glasgow, Scotland's largest city, and to this day welcomes any player willing to pony up the £165 greens fee.

The links course at Prestwick, the site of the first British Open (1860), the oldest of the majors, still uses six of the original greens and three complete holes that Old Tom Morris played during his two-shot victory in the second Open. Aye, Morris had a bit of local knowledge, having designed Prestwick's links and served as the greenskeeper and maker of clubs and balls there since 1854. But there probably weren't two dozen courses in the world at the time, so every accomplished player had ties to at least one of them. Old Tom was from St. Andrews, and went to work back there after his first Open victory, but he would return to Prestwick to help expand the course from its original twelve holes—they played three times around on consecutive days in early Opens—to the eighteen that became standard.

By 1925, Prestwick had hosted the Open twenty-four times; Morris's son, Young Tom Morris, who played there as a boy, would win four. But the tight layout couldn't accommodate the growing galleries, and Prestwick was removed from the Open rotation after 1925, when the spectators overwhelmed the few marshals on hand and disrupted play. Thanks in part to those hooligan golf fans, you can make a starting time at Prestwick, one of Old Tom's early masterpieces, and walk the links that are among the game's oldest and most beloved survivors.

The hazards facing Ian Campbell in 2001, like those confronting Old Tom Morris a century earlier, are part of Prestwick's classic beauty.

LAKERS' SHOWTIME

WHERE: *Staples Center, Los Angeles, California*
WHEN: *October to April*

WHY: EVEN NOW, WATCHING THE LAKERS RUN OUT ON THE break, it's impossible not to flash back to Showtime, that brand of basketball that brought a string of championships to LA and unprecedented glamour and excitement to the NBA.

No one would mistake the Lakers of recent vintage for the team built around the NBA's paradigm-shifting point guard and its all-time leading scorer—Magic and Kareem, a pair of one-name wonders for the ages. When he bought the Lakers in 1979, Jerry Buss brought show biz to the hardwood as never before, surrounding his high-scoring, fast-breaking Lakers with music and movie stars and, not least, a sea of flowing locks and Lycra known far and wide as the Laker Girls. This was Showtime, a hybrid of pro hoops and Hollywood, and under coach Pat Riley, the Lakers won five NBA titles in the eighties and helped propel the league to the center of the popular culture.

The original Showtime, of course, left the building long ago. In 1999, after thirty-two years at the Fabulous Forum, the Lakers moved to the Staples Center. Shaq and Kobe, running Phil Jackson's more deliberate triangle offense, would win three more NBA titles before a long dry spell set in. But when you sit in Staples and peer through the Laker Girls and survey the home team's bench—and, yes, that's Jack Nicholson in his usual seat—you might notice that, wafting above the gold and purple, there's still an unmistakable tang of Showtime in the air.

The word Showtime will always conger up images not just of Kareem and Magic on the break, but of Lakers Girls at center stage and of Jack courtside.

THE FIELD OF DREAMS

WHERE: *Dyersville, Iowa*
WHEN: *Summer*

WHY: THIS TINY DIAMOND IN AN IOWA CORNFIELD, created as a set for the 1989 movie *Field of Dreams*, spontaneously grew into a baseball mecca, the power of which has barely abated almost thirty years later. What is it that compels people to drive great distances to lay eyes on a little ball field carved out of farmland as the make-believe scene of a supernatural baseball flick?

Well, first and foremost, there was the movie: an Oscar nominee for best picture, it was a story of fathers and sons, of guilt and redemption and baseball—a cornball classic, and hugely popular (notwithstanding Richard Corliss of *Time*, who famously called it a "male weepie at its wussiest").

It touched a nerve, and that nerve just kept firing. During its heyday in the nineties, the field was one of Iowa's top tourist attractions—among the competition: the nearby National Farm Toy Museum, and the World of Checkers Museum in Dubuque—drawing upward of 65,000 visitors a year. In those days, members of a local semipro team would emerge in uniform from the cornfield, just as the ghosts of disgraced players did in the movie, and toss a ball around.

The appeal of the field and the cottage industry it spawned have been remarkably resilient. But the diamond lies on land that was sold in 2013 to Chicago developers, whose plan for a giant sports complex spawned local opposition. So far, the field remains and the pilgrims keep coming, but don't assume that the supernatural powers of baseball can keep it there forever.

The players who emerge from the cornfield in Dyersville are just movie reenactors, but the Field of Dreams *magic is very much alive.*

PERMIAN PANTHERS FOOTBALL

WHERE: *Ratliff Stadium, Odessa, Texas*
WHEN: *Friday nights, Autumn*

WHY: THE BELOVED BOOK *FRIDAY NIGHT LIGHTS* BY BUZZ Bissinger, and the movie and TV series it inspired, were based on the Permian Panthers, a quintessential Texas high school football team, and the culture that surrounds them. The real Panthers still play their home games at Ratliff Stadium (where football scenes for the 2004 movie were shot), but the storyline has veered sharply from the one that made Permian, for good or ill, the object of intense scrutiny.

The storied world of Texas schoolboy football hardly began with Bissinger's book. In fact, it was Permian's success—four state championships between 1965 and 1984—that caught the author's eye when he wanted to write about the phenomenon. His book, which follows the town and its team through the drive for the 1988 state championship, was a huge hit when it was published in 1990—except in Odessa, where there was an immediate and vicious backlash. While no one disputed the central role of football and its powerful effect on the community, many felt betrayed by Bissinger's unsparing glimpses of racism and misguided priorities.

Meanwhile, as the oil-and-gas economy of Odessa has endured the boom-and-bust cycles of the past twenty-five years, Permian football has done likewise. The Panthers have yet to repeat that 1988 championship, and the obsession might have ebbed a bit, but if you have the slightest doubt that high school football and its "clear eyes, full hearts, can't lose" culture is alive and well in Texas, head out to Ratliff Stadium on Friday nights in the fall, when Permian plays under the lights.

Texas was devoted to schoolboy football long before Friday Night Lights, *and the fervor is still felt in Permian, where the story began.*

IRONMAN WORLD CHAMPIONSHIPS

WHERE: *Kailua-Kona, Hawaii*
WHEN: *October 13, 2018*

WHY: THE ULTIMATE TEST OF THE ENDURANCE ATHLETE, the Ironman championship is extreme sport amid the extreme beauty of the Kona coast of Hawaii. Not that the 2.4-mile rough-water swim, 112-mile bike ride, and a 26.2-mile run leave much time or energy for sightseeing. But even if you're strictly a spectator, there to bear witness to the dedication and courage of athletes who are testing their limits, can you imagine a better place than Kailua for a triathlon?

When it kicked off in 1978 with all of fifteen participants, the Ironman World Championship was a novel challenge for runners and cyclists and swimmers who thought a mere marathon or hundred-mile bike race wasn't nearly enough. The idea spread quickly—it didn't hurt when the Ironman was featured on ABC's Wide World of Sports in 1980—appealing to an aspirational streak common to many endurance athletes.

The championships now include more than 2,300 competitors annually, divided into pro and amateur classes and age groups, which ensures a wide range of abilities. Because competition is intense for a starting spot in Hawaii, entry is limited mostly to those who qualify in various regional Ironman events (with some additional spots determined by lottery or purchased for charity). And though the event boasts more than $600,000 in prize money and the Ironman mantra is "Anything Is Possible!" very few "pros" can actually earn a living at it; more than 75 percent earn less than $10,000 a year. Dedication is the name of this game, and the spectacle is all the better because it is so clearly not about winning the dough.

It's a staggering sight when a couple thousand athletes set out on their 2.4 mile rough-water swim, the first leg of the Ironman.

Going To Extremes

Five other events to test the limits of overambitious endurance athletes

Marathon de Sables

A hellish ultra-run through Saharan heat and terrain in Morocco—the equivalent of six marathons in six days

Coureur des Bois

Cross-country skiing for 100 miles in the dead of the Canadian winter, roughly from Montreal to Ottawa

Iditarod Trail Invitational

A thousand miles through Alaska on foot, bike, sled, or skis, in February, carrying all your own supplies, with a 30-day limit

Badwater Ultra-Marathon

A 135-mile summer run from California's Death Valley (temperatures above 120) to the Mt. Whitney trailhead (altitude about 8000 feet)

Race Across America

An annual 3,000-mile bike race, from west to east, open to individuals or alternating teams (up to 8 riders), with a 14-day limit. Solo riders can pedal through 20-hour days.

A 112-mile ride begins on the Kona coast and leads straight to a 26.2-mile run that, in and of itself, is often considered the ultimate test of stamina.

KENTUCKY VS. LOUISVILLE

WHERE: *Rupp Arena, Lexington, or KFC Yum! Center, Louisville*

WHEN: *Late December through early January*

WHY: THESE SCHOOLS ARE FEWER THAN EIGHTY MILES apart in a state that has no major pro sports team and takes basketball very seriously. Both teams are part of the hoops elite, having combined for 27 Final Four appearances and 11 national championships. The two coaches have much in common, too, including NBA experience and NCAA titles, and though they are both among the state's highest-paid employees, they are not, let us say, best of friends. In fact, they are Cats and Cardinals, natural rivals if not born enemies.

You could go further and just call this one of the top rivalries in all of college sports. Kentucky, coached by John Calipari, has won more games than any team in NCAA history (2,207 through 2015–2016, and counting) and has eight national championships to show for it, most recently in 2012 and 2014. And guess who won that title in between, in 2013? Why, it was Louisville, coached by Rick Pitino (who also won the title at Kentucky in 1996).

Both schools attract a steady stream of top-flight talent, which has made them reliable tributaries to the NBA (they had produced a combined 174 NBA draft picks through 2015). They also play their home games at two of the three biggest hoops-only arenas in the United States. Since the KFC Yum! Center (capacity: 22,800) opened in 2010, the Cardinals have rarely disappointed the crowds, winning almost 80 percent of their games there. Kentucky's Rupp Arena packs in a few more (23,500), and the Cats win at home just as often (89.2 percent). It's the perfect rivalry: two great teams, both college hoops royalty, destined to play out their eternal feud at dueling basketball palaces.

Whether it's in Lexington (opposite) or Louisville, the rivalry between Pitino (left) and Calipari is as fierce as the one between their teams.

OLYMPICS OPENING CEREMONIES

WHERE: *National Olympic Stadium, Tokyo, Japan*
WHEN: *July 24, 2020*

WHY: THE PHYSICAL DEMANDS OF THE OPENING ceremonies on Olympic athletes are limited to parade walking and occasional cap tipping, but the grandeur and pageantry that kick off the games are unlike any other in sports. Which is exactly what the International Olympic Committee (IOC) has in mind.

As the Lords of the Rings readily declare, "It is the ceremonial aspects of the Olympic Games that set them apart." What the IOC does not mention in this context is that the Olympic TV rights go for billions of dollars, and the organizers want to ensure that no one in the world within a half-day's walk of a Wi-Fi signal will fail to know that the games are under way and available for viewing. Accordingly, IOC Rule 55 prescribes a detailed protocol for the opening ceremony, which includes the host country's head of state formally kicking off the show. And sure enough, everyone from King George I (Athens, 1896) to Adolf Hitler (Berlin, 1936) to Queen Elizabeth II (London, 2012), has done the honors. You'd think such a recipe by Olympic bureaucrats might cook the life out of this ritual. But you'd be wrong.

The show opener in Beijing in 2008, the ultimate expression of Olympic pageantry, used 22,000 actors in a celebration of China's history and culture, all infused with the benign nationalism that is the pumping heart of international sports. The lid lifter in London in 2012 emulated Beijing, but with Brazil mired in recession, the pendulum swung back toward moderation at the Rio games. Don't bet that Beijing's spectacle will stand unchallenged, though—not until you see the games open in Japan.

The pomp and pageantry of the Olympic kick-off in London aimed, as always, to grab the world's attention, a job it did well.

EMPIRE STATE RUN-UP

WHERE: *New York, New York*
WHEN: *February*

WHY: IT SOUNDS LIKE SOMETHING YOU'D DO ONLY ON A dare: race up 86 floors, 1,576 steps, in a lung-searing ten- or twelve-minute sprint from the lobby to the top of New York's classic art deco skyscraper. But the Towerrunning World Tour bills this annual dash as "the pinnacle event in global tower racing," always attracting what it calls the world's top professionals.

Who even knew there was such a sport as tower running, much less a world tour? Well, it's true (though "professional" might be stretching it a bit; most races include heats for amateurs). There are more than two hundred tower running events every year, which usually involve skyscrapers but can include other man-made structures with lots of stairs. The biggest of these are the fifteen or so Masters Events, the ones on that world tour, which has stops in a dozen cities, from Paris to Guangzhou.

The Empire State event is—pardon the expression—top flight. The brainchild of Fred Lebow, a cofounder of the New York Marathon, it has been run for almost forty years and always attracts an international field and lots of attention. As the race grew in stature, it became harder to get in the door, either to watch or to run. Security concerns post-9/11 intensified that trend. These days, the best way to ensure you'll get in is to whip yourself into shape and see those endless stairwells from the inside, as a tower runner. Of course, you'll want to avoid the elite heats, but you can actually get into this game by qualifying at an earlier event, by winning a lottery, or by applying for one of the charity heats. You've got to really want it. Either that, or you can do it on a dare.

The grueling sprint up 1,576 steps thins the herd that starts racing in the lobby and finishes on the observation deck, 102 floors above.

FOOTBALL AT WEST POINT

WHERE: *Michie Stadium, West Point, N.Y.*
WHEN: *Autumn*

WHY: PERCHED ON A HILL OVERLOOKING THE HUDSON river and much of the stately West Point campus, Michie Stadium seems far grander than its seating capacity (38,000) and vintage (1924) might suggest. True, it's been a long time since Army football was in the top echelon of the college game—since the Black Knights won three straight national championships (from 1944 to 1946) and regularly fielded players who were household names (Doc Blanchard, Glenn Davis, and Pete Dawkins, Heisman winners and American icons all); and it's been ages since even Army-Navy was on every fan's list of can't-miss games. But a fall Saturday at West Point remains to this day a college football feast like no other—an irresistible amalgam of homecoming weekend and the Fourth of July.

It starts in earnest three hours before kickoff, with the full-dress parade of cadets on the Plain. This leaves plenty of time for a leisurely stroll across campus, a stop in the West Point museum, and an eyeful of the Hudson Valley, aflame with fall leaves. But be in your seat in Michie in time to see the cadets, a thousand strong, take the field along with the Army band and glee club for a stirring performance of the national anthem. Want more? Cue the paratroopers who drop from helicopters to deliver the game ball. The energy doesn't slacken after kickoff, either, as 4,000 cadets stand, chanting and cheering, throughout the game. They've been doing this stuff at Army football games for more than one hundred seasons, and if you've got a patriotic bone in your body, you'll understand instantly why it never gets old.

The scene at Michie Stadium on fall Saturdays is as rousing now as it was in 1989, when the cadet corps sensed an Army victory in the air.

BARCELONA VS. REAL MADRID

WHERE: *Camp Nou, Barcelona, Spain*
WHEN: *October to May (La Liga)*
plus other dates (Copa del Rey, UEFA)

WHY: IN A CITY OF ARCHITECTURAL SPLENDORS LIKE GAUDÍ'S Sagrada Famíla and the Casa Milà, Camp Nou, Europe's largest soccer stadium, is a comparatively bland-looking edifice. But inside await the wonders of Lionel Messi and the great Barcelona Football Club he leads. So strong is Barca and so loud the 95,354 fans who routinely turn out at Nou that when opponents make their way from the dressing room to the pitch, they sometimes stop for help at a room that beckons on their right, a small chapel.

But praying hasn't been enough. During the Messi era—though the monolith has shown recent signs of erosion—there has been no more aesthetically pleasing brand of soccer in the world than the fluid, one-touch, tiqui-taka style that Barca uses to pass opponents into submission. Barca's supremacy came to full flower in 2010, when the team won its third straight Liga title and Spain won the World Cup starting six Barca players.

If there's one team that always has much more than a prayer of beating Barca, it's Real Madrid, the most popular soccer club in Spain and the most valuable in the world (Barcelona ranks a close second on both counts). Led by the incomparable Cristiano Ronaldo, Real has won 32 Liga titles (to Barca's 24), and a record 11 Euro championships.

Whenever these titans meet, the game is El Clasico, a rivalry that transcends sports and embodies the deep political and cultural rift between Catalonians (Barcelona) and Castilians (Madrid). That may help interpret the section of seat backs in Camp Nou that spell out Barca's motto, *Mes que un club*. More than a club.

Soccer loyalties are woven into Spain's culture, with rivalries played out in El Clasico, whenever Ronaldo and his Madrid team face Barcelona.

NCAA MEN'S FINAL FOUR

WHERE: *San Antonio (2018), Minneapolis (2019) and Atlanta (2020), Indianapolis (2021)*
WHEN: *Late March*

WHY: SINCE THE COLLEGE BASKETBALL TOURNAMENT expanded to 64 teams in 1985—two additional play-in games further fattened the field to 68 in 2011—March Madness has grown into the only nationwide sports phenomenon in a class with the Super Bowl. But while Super Sunday is merely a single national holiday, the NCAAs are a three-week blitz of do-or-die, elimination games, with ubiquitous office pools and "expert" analysts who have overrun the media landscape like an invasive species. The number of broadcast and online viewers has also exploded—the 2016 final drew an average TV audience of 17.8 million homes, while live streaming doubled previous rates and records. As fans stormed that bandwagon in vast numbers, rocketing rights fees have made the tournament worth more than $1 billion a year to the NCAA.

But hasn't the blanket TV coverage hurt live attendance? Since 2009, the NCAA has required that the Final Four site be an indoor dome that can hold 70,000 for basketball. In 2016, in Houston, the Final drew 74,340. Even in those huge arenas, the scene is always both collegiate and electric, with brassy bands, acrobatic cheerleaders, and faithful fans of all ages who are fully charged for the climatic games of the season. You'd think it would be tough to get a ticket to the final, despite all that seating capacity, right? But about half the fans who follow their teams to the Final Four will see them lose in Saturday's semifinals, and many pack up their broken hearts, unload their seats for Monday's final, and head for home. Their crushing loss is your good fortune—your ticket to the final.

In 2016, America's annual case of March Madness peaked when Villanova beat Oklahoma in the semis (right), then Carolina in the final.

THE OLD COURSE

WHERE: *St. Andrews, Scotland*
WHEN: *April to October (high season)*

WHY: IN WHAT MIGHT'VE BEEN THE GREATEST TRIPADVISOR review of all time, one deeply experienced traveler to St. Andrews had this to say: "If I had to select one course upon which to play the match of my life, I should have selected the Old Course."

That opinion isn't quite as old as the course itself, but its source was none other than Bobby Jones, who first played there in the 1921 British Open—after taking four futile swings in a bunker on the 11th hole, Jones walked off the course—but who returned in 1930 to win the British Amateur. He also, by the way, founded Augusta National. All to say, he knew a thing or two about golf and didn't blame those four bad bunker shots on his clubs or the course.

By anyone's measure, the Old Course at St. Andrews has much to recommend it. Established in 1552 and with Old Tom Morris as its guiding light for almost forty years, it had an enormous influence on golf's development through the early twentieth century. Four of the original twenty-two holes at St. Andrews, for instance, were deemed too short and combined into four, leaving the eighteen that emerged as the game's standard. Other of its features have likewise become iconic: the 700-year-old Swilken Bridge and the Royal and Ancient clubhouse, an exclusive private club adjacent to the first tee, but whose members hold no special playing privileges.

One of the best things about the Old Course, after all, is that it's public. So if you can't wait for the thirtieth British Open there in 2020, just go to standrews.com and make a tee time for yourself. And don't forget to write a review.

Rory McIlroy, hitting his tee shot on No. 18 at St. Andrews in 2010, would have to wait another four years to win his first British Open.

THE AMERICA'S CUP

WHERE: *Bermuda*

WHEN: *June 2017*

WHY: THE AMERICA'S CUP WASN'T ALWAYS "A BILLIONAIRE'S death race," which is only one of the things it's been called since the old mono-hulled yachts of the late twentieth century morphed into the hydrofoiling, wing-sailed catamarans that now fly across the water at Marvel Comics speeds.. It can't be denied, though, that the Cup has always inspired a competitive madness the likes of which are rarely seen, even in sports.

It all started when the schooner America won an ugly silver trophy in a match race around the Isle of Wight in 1851. The United States retained that cup through twenty-six challenges over the next 132 years, then lost it for the first time, to Australia, in 1983. Soon, what had been just a rarefied sailing race escalated into a technological cold war. And when Larry Ellison, the founder of Oracle, got into the game in 2003, he began building boats faster and more advanced than anything seen before. All you really need to know is that in 2007, the average top speed for an America's Cup boat, a state-of-the-art racing machine, was roughly 11.5 miles per hour; in the successful US defense in 2013, that figure was 46 miles per hour. During preparations for those races, a crewmember drowned when one of the hot new AC72 wing-sailed catamarans went over in the high winds off San Francisco. Amid much soul-searching and debate, the show went on, but not without calls for de-escalation, which led to slightly smaller but still incredibly fast boats the next time around.

Back in the day, when the United States never lost the Cup, defender trials were predictably held off Newport, Rhode Island, every four years. Now the defender and challenger trials are branded together as the Louis Vuitton America's Cup World Series, which give landlubbers all over the world a choice: catch a glimpse of these wondrous, surface-skimming speed machines, or risk being left behind in a world where racing boats are still stuck in the water.

Barely touching the water at times, Oracle Team USA retained the Cup by beating New Zealand in stiff winds off San Francisco in 2013.

HARLEM GLOBETROTTERS

WHERE: *Throughout the United States and Europe*
WHEN: *More than 200 times per year*

WHY: FOR MORE THAN NINETY YEARS, THE GLOBIES HAVE been touring the world with their patented blend of razzle-dazzle basketball and comic theater, their signature routines—the balls spun crazily on fingertips, the intricate weaves and superhuman dribbling tricks—performed to the familiar whistled tune of "Sweet Georgia Brown." It's an act that appeals to the kid in all of us, but unlike us, it never gets old.

If you doubt for a moment their hoops cred, consider that such NBA names as Wilt Chamberlain, Connie Hawkins, and Sweetwater Clifton played in Globetrotters' uniforms. Not convinced? Well, the analytics website FiveThirtyEight took an unsentimental look at how good the Globies really are. Based on a substantial series of games they played against Division 1 college teams between 2000 and 2003, the number crunchers concluded that a typical Globetrotters squad is roughly equivalent to a fourth- or fifth-seeded NCAA tournament team. Not Wilt the Stilt level, perhaps, but hardly a bunch of clowns.

Statistics, however—even serious analytics—are extra slippery when you're talking about a team that since 1927 has played more than 25,000 exhibition games in more than 120 countries against a wide range of opponents. Throughout the 1950s, the Globetrotters played against NBA squads. But from 1953 to 2015, their most frequent "opponent" was the Washington Generals, who faced them some 13,000 times, winning six. The Generals were paid to play the games, not win them. As their player-coach Red Klotz once said, "Beating the Globetrotters is like shooting Santa Claus."

For roughly 90 years, the Globetrotters have been doing just that, delighting fans around the world with their dazzling athletic theater.

DOUBLEDAY FIELD

WHERE: *Cooperstown, New York*
WHEN: *Hall of Fame weekend, late July*

WHY: ACCORDING TO BASEBALL MYTHOLOGY, ABNER Doubleday invented the game in 1839 at the current site of his eponymous field, which just happens to be a two-block stroll from the economic mainspring of Cooperstown, the National Baseball Hall of Fame— the greatest of all sports halls. To visit the gem of a ballpark built in Doubleday's honor is to give yourself over completely to the game's mythology as well as its actual history. So go ahead, because Cooperstown, like many great movies and books, at times requires a suspension of disbelief that somehow makes it all the more authentic.

The full-immersion experience of Cooperstown takes place during induction weekend; for many years that was when they played the Hall of Fame Game, a high-profile MLB exhibition, until it faded from the schedule. Now, whether the baseball is played by MLB old-timers (as it is on induction weekend) or your office softball team (Doubleday can be rented for about $500), the place has a deeply evocative charm. As does the hall itself.

The legend of Doubleday as baseball's inventor and of Cooperstown as its birthplace was heavily promoted by the town's Chamber of Commerce to establish it as the game's ancestral home. So in some real sense, the hall was built on a myth. But the institution that has grown there is a treasured repository of baseball's history. As such, the hall long ago inducted Alexander Cartwright as baseball's true inventor. But if recently discovered documents prove authentic and a man named Doc Adams actually invented the game, Cartwright may soon be the new Abner Doubleday.

For many years the home of MLB's Hall of Fame game, Doubleday retains its charm as it hosts less monumental games in Cooperstown.

RYERSON RAMS HOCKEY

WHERE: *Mattamy Athletic Centre, Toronto, Canada*
WHEN: *October to February*

WHY: THE MATTAMY CENTRE IS NOW THE HOME OF THE Ryerson University hockey team, but for most of the years after its opening in 1931, it was a cathedral to hockey and the home to one of the NHL's Original Six. Does "Maple Leaf Gardens" ring a bell?

The arena was long a beacon of national pride. It was built in seven months in the heart of Toronto, and it remains, as they say, "in the hearts of Canadians." The Leafs won the Stanley Cup in its inaugural season, and ten more times by 1967 (but never again while they resided there, until 1999). It hosted the first NHL All-Star Game. Churchill spoke there in 1932. The Beatles appeared there on all three of their North American tours. Muhammad Ali beat George Chuvalo there in 1966. The building was declared a Canadian National Historic Site in 2007.

A major renovation, begun in 2009, gutted the Gardens but preserved the historic exterior, and a new hockey rink was constructed, of precisely the same size and on the same spot. As the centerpiece of the Mattamy Centre, the Rams' home ice seats a cozy 2,796, with a cozy irony to match: The owners of the Maple Leafs sued Ryerson to prevent the university from using the Gardens' original name. The only remaining declaration of the building's provenance is the marquee over Carlton Street. The Leafs, meanwhile, have gone from the pride of Toronto to the butt of national jokes, with an ongoing Stanley Cup drought that began in 1967. According to Forbes, however, the Leafs remain the most valuable sports franchise in Canada, not to mention the NHL. And their old Gardens, whatever you call them, are thriving as well.

The Mattamy Center, Ryerson College's home ice, hosted the NHL Legends game in 2013, recalling its sacred place in Maple Leaf's lore.

JAYHAWKS AT ALLEN FIELDHOUSE

WHERE: *Lawrence, Kansas*
WHEN: *November to March*

WHY: BECAUSE OF THE CONSISTENT QUALITY OF THE TEAM and the history that permeates the place, the home of University of Kansas basketball is considered by many to be the single best place to see high-end college hoops. The Jayhawks' home court is named for Phog Allen, the so-called father of basketball coaching. Indeed, the place is sort of a fertile crescent of college basketball, the ancestral home of players and coaches and teams that represent the very foundation of the sport.

Consider just this little bit of lineage: as a player at Kansas, Phog Allen himself was coached by James Naismith, who merely invented basketball, and Allen in turn coached (among many others) Adolph Rupp and Dean Smith, who would grow into major branches of the coaching tree that overarches the college and pro game. (And add this bit of trivia to win a postgame beer: Naismith is the only Kansas coach to this day to have a losing record.)

OK, so the place is a living museum. What about Jayhawks basketball itself? Well, it's true, Kansas has made it to only 14 Final Fours and has won only three NCAA titles. And only 21 first-team All-Americans (the most of any school) have come through the program, which is represented by only 19 active players in the NBA. And hey, it's been a long time since Wilt Chamberlain dominated everyone he played against at KU, though the Jayhawks have somehow managed to go 700-108 (.866) at Allen Fieldhouse (including, at one point, 69 wins in a row) since it opened in 1955. Still and all, you're assured of seeing one of the most famous, if nonsensical, cheers in college hoops—the "Rock, Chalk, Jayhawk" chant—and, with any luck at all, some pretty good basketball.

Andrew Wiggens (22) and Wayne Selden (1) are among the many Jayhawks stars who prepped for the NBA by lighting it up at Allen.

THE SUPER BOWL

WHERE: *Minneapolis, Minnesota* (LII); *Atlanta, Georgia* (LIII)
WHEN: *February 2018* (LII); *February 2019* (LIII)

WHY: WHAT CAN WE POSSIBLY SAY ABOUT A GAME THAT, fifty years on, is already a national celebration of football and TV commercials and halftime entertainment that would make Vegas blush, and that just keeps getting bigger? Well, we can say, as they always do, that it offers the world's most expensive minutes of TV ad time. And with only one exception since 2000, the audience viewing those ads (and the game) will be bigger than it was a year earlier. That's true whether it's Seattle's 43–8 blowout of Denver in 2014, a dog of a game that drew an average of 112.2 million viewers, or New England's teeth-gnashing 28–24 win over Seattle a year later, one of the best Super Bowls ever and the highest-rated show in TV history (114.4 million US viewers).

While everyone *watches* the Super Bowl, getting tickets can be trickier. The face value ranges from about $850 to $1,800. But demand always dwarfs supply, so, according to SeatGeek.com, expect to pay between $2,500 and $3,000 these days for "get-in-the-door" tickets. The highest average price in history, for Super Bowl 50, was $4,639. If you want to play the market, be aware that prices tend to rise through the week leading up to the game, peaking on Saturday; that means you can sometimes find a relative bargain on game day, but not always: In Santa Clara (near all those Silicon Valley billions) in 2016, tickets were so scarce on Super Bowl Sunday that they went for $9,000 and up. With hype and expectation always turned up to eleven, the biggest game is often a big letdown. But everyone wants to go, of course, and if you get lucky and see a classic, it's worth any price—maybe even nine grand.

Brady led the Pats to their fourth Lombardi Trophy—and was the game's MVP for the third time—with a thrilling win over Seattle in 2015.

Peyton Manning (above) won his second title in 2016; James Harrison (opposite) returned a pick 100 yards in Pittsburgh's win in SB XLIII.

The Wagers of Sin

Super Bowl has long been the most gambled-on event in America. Here are some of the best and worst bets ever, judging by the point spread.

BIGGEST UPSETS

Super Bowl/Matchup	Line	Winner	Score
III COLTS-JETS	Colts-18	Jets	16-7
XXXVI PATRIOTS-RAMS	Rams-14	Patriots	20-17
XLII PATRIOTS-GIANTS	Patriots-12	Giants	17-14
IV CHIEFS-VIKINGS	Vikings-12	Chiefs	23-7
XXXII BRONCOS-PACKERS	Packers-11	Broncos	34-19

SUREST BETS

Super Bowl/Matchup	Line	Winner	Score
XXIX NINERS-CHARGERS	Niners-18.5	Niners	49-26
I PACKERS-CHIEFS	Packers-14	Packers	35-10
XXXI PACKERS-PATRIOTS	Packers-14	Packers	35-21
XXXIV TITANS-STL.RAMS	Rams-7	Rams	23-16
XIV STEELERS-L.A.RAMS	Steelers-10.5	Steelers	31-19

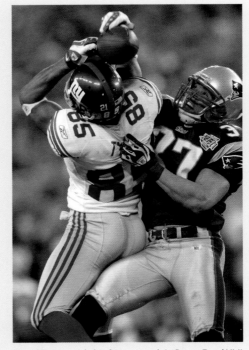

David Tyree made his famous grab in Super Bowl XLII.

THE BOAT RACE

WHERE: *River Thames, London, England*
WHEN: *March-April (around Easter)*

WHY: ONE OF THE REMARKABLE THINGS ABOUT VISITING England is that so much of what you see is steeped in history and tangled legend, not to mention class and lineage. Take this annual race between heavy-weight eights, for instance: crews from Oxford and Cambridge, rowing a 4.2-mile course on the Thames in West London. A major point of honor between Great Britain's two great universities, it was first run in 1829, after Charles Wordsworth (nephew of William), an Oxford man, met Charles Merivale of Cambridge (son of the master of Eton). The two chaps went rowing on the Cam and cooked up a challenge pitting boats from their universities to be run the following Easter vacation. It was all very civilized. And thus it has remained.

Which is not to say there has been no controversy in the 162 races that have ensued. There was that frightful mess in 1912, when both boats sank in stormy weather. And, of course, there was that clash of oar blades in 2004 (begun by Oxford, it is widely agreed), and that bloody swimmer who had the audacity to interfere with the Oxford boat during the race in 2012.

While many traditions abide, much has changed: the cutting-edge boat and oar technology, the modern training and world-class athletes (most notably Matthew Pinsent, who twice won for Oxford before winning four Olympic golds for queen and country). And since 2015, the quarter-million spectators who line the Thames on race day always fancy those other two boats, the women's eights, that fight it out on a second front of this ancient war.

Oxford's crew led as the boats passed under Hammersmith Bridge in 2016, but Cambridge would win this 161st renewal of the classic race.

THE KING OF CLEVELAND

WHERE: *Quicken Loans Arena, Cleveland, Ohio*
WHEN: *ASAP*

WHY: THIS IS ONE OF THOSE GET-IT-WHILE-YOU-CAN DEALS: hurry to an arena, any NBA arena, where the best player of his era is appearing during the late laps of his career—a run that has been astonishing even if it was deemed a sure thing back in the day when King James was just a bible.

While we calculate our chances of getting one more look at LeBron James in action, let's recall very briefly how this fairy tale unfolded before our eyes: The son of a sixteen-year-old single mom who raised him alone, he won every possible accolade as a high school star in Akron, appearing on Sports Illustrated's cover as a junior, billed as the Chosen One. Taken by Cleveland with the first draft pick in 2003, he was NBA Rookie of the Year at nineteen. Six more seasons as a Cav, two MVPs later, he made the lamented Decision and took his talents to Miami, incurring the wrath of fans everywhere. Playing the villain the next four years, he led the Heat to four finals and two NBA titles, with two more MVPs. Then came redemption with the return of the prodigal son to Cleveland, where his first two years yielded two finals and the Cavs' first title, an unprecedented comeback against the next Chosen One, Stephen Curry, and his Warriors, coming off the best NBA season ever. All, it seemed, was forgiven.

Along the way, he spoke his mind on controversial issues and still managed to make a fortune in endorsements to match the one he made on the court—a net worth estimated in 2016 at $300 million. You can't make this stuff up, but it's still hard to believe it's true. So you better see it with your own eyes, while you can.

A Game 7 block of Stephen Curry was just one inspired play from the highlight reel of LeBron's MVP performance in the 2016 Finals.

THE CHAMPIONSHIPS AT WIMBLEDON

WHERE: *All England Lawn Tennis and Croquet Club, London, England*

WHEN: *Late June to early July*

WHY: THE OLDEST TENNIS TOURNAMENT IN THE WORLD (1877) remains the favorite of many longtime tennis fans because it has adapted to the demands of the modern world while retaining a crucial measure of its Old World charm. It's the last of the Grand Slams still played on grass, of course, and they still serve strawberries and cream (60,000 pounds of the former, 7,500 quarts of the latter, at last count). And though players are now allowed tiny colored accents on their tennis whites, they still bow or curtsy when the queen is in the Royal Box. The big titles are still called the gentlemen's and ladies' singles, though the prize money is the same for both, as is good and proper.

There are other conspicuous nods to modernity at Wimbledon, not least of them the retractable roof over Centre Court. Which is not to say that rain can't still interfere with the overall draw—only Centre Court can be covered, and even there it takes twenty minutes for the roof to roll into place, leaving plenty of time for a lawn-soaking downpour. But back in the day when Martina Navratilova was winning her record nine singles titles and Pete Sampras his seven (a feat equaled only by Roger Federer, so far), there were none of these niceties to protect players from the elements.

Another technological leap forward is the giant TV that was installed so fans could watch important matches from the grassy hill known officially as Aorangi Terrace. You'll probably want to queue up for a ticket to the big singles finals on Centre Court, but if you don't get lucky in that line, it's all quite civilized on the grass, in front of the giant TV.

Among the many pleasures of the Championships at Wimbledon are the strawberries and cream that traditionally accompany the tennis.

HEAVYWEIGHT TITLE FIGHT

WHERE: *Las Vegas, Nevada*
WHEN: *To Be Determined*

WHY: IT'S ONE OF THE OLDEST CLICHÉS IN SPORTS, WHICH puts it in a class with Rocky: as the heavyweights go, so goes boxing. And not since Mike Tyson struck fear into the hearts of men everywhere (and the occasional woman) has boxing's glamour division commanded worldwide attention. But there are signs of life in the Sweet Science, and when a classic heavyweight bout finally comes along, don't miss it, because there is nothing in sports like the electricity that crackles through the air when two big men with bad intentions enter the ring.

From the current vantage point, it's hard to recall the era of Ali or even Tyson, when boxing wasn't just mainstream sport, it was transcendent. In Ali's wake, the sport was balkanized into competing alphabet organizations—WBC, WBO, IBF, ad nauseam—their title belts fractured and devalued. A devolving business sought marketable boxers to sell, and so bred generations of undefeated contenders who fed on inferior opponents cherry-picked from the rankings. The public gradually lost interest, leaving a huge opening for the rise of mixed martial arts.

Oh how far the heavyweight division had fallen when the brightest glimmer of hope was a unified champion called Tyson Fury. Although blessed with neither Ali's supreme skill nor Tyson's mesmerizing power, Fury was a mouthy showboater with a shot at rekindling broader interest. And with China looming as a land of pugilistic promise, and Cuba finally back in the game, it may not be long before we have a world heavyweight champion worthy of the name and a title bout the whole world will have to watch.

The days may yet return when a champ like Tyson (staggering Tony Tubbs in 1988) made every title bout a worldwide, must-see event.

MEXICO VS. U.S.A. SOCCER

WHERE: *Stadium Azteca, Mexico City; or the Rose Bowl, Pasadena, California*
WHEN: *To be determined*

WHY: ALTHOUGH THE US AND MEXICAN NATIONAL TEAMS have a history that reaches back to a 1934 World Cup qualifier, it was only when the United States began to feel a consistantly competitive side in the 1990s that the rivalry became extra hot and spicy. Whether they face off in the 104,000-seat Estadio Azteca, the host of two World Cup finals, or the venerable Rose Bowl, the site of the 1999 Women's World Cup final (a.k.a. the Brandi Chastain sports bra game), this is now a must-see match.

The early years of the rivalry were, of course, dominated by Mexico, which still leads the series by a wide margin. Before 2012, Mexico had never lost to the Yanks at home. But since 2000, the United States has actually had the upper hand, going 13-6-5 (through 2015), especially on home soil

So why is home turf such a powerful advantage, even as the strength of the national teams has evened out? Well, for one thing, there's the business of the urine. At Azteca, visiting players are routinely bombarded with plastic bags of urine. In the case of the gringos, this probably has something to do with a practice session for an Olympic qualifying match in Guadalajara in 2004, during which the US star Landon Donovan was reported in the Mexican press to have relieved himself on the field. Mexican fans took special offense at this, though a video—there's always a video now—later showed Donovan watering some bushes that were actually outside the practice area. No matter: this is the kind of stuff that can piss great nations off, the stuff of which rivalries are made. Just add vinegar and decades of ill will.

Whether it's in the Rose Bowl (left) or Azteca Stadium in Mexico City, US-Mexico matches always ignite the passions of players and fans alike.

THE BOSTON MARATHON

WHERE: *Boston, Massachusetts*
WHEN: *Patriot's Day (the third Monday in April)*

WHY: AMERICA'S OLDEST AND BEST-KNOWN MARATHON (first run in 1897, and in every year since), Boston is limited to about 38,000 runners, and its diabolical changes in elevation put to the test even those who can meet its qualifying standards. But half a million spectators always turn out to cheer the runners, and the 2013 bombings—and Boston Strong, the city's defiant response—somehow made this venerable springtime ritual all the more inspiring.

Obviously, the only way to experience every mile of the marathon is to be out there on the roads of eastern Massachusetts running it: From the start in Hopkinton, down into Ashland (and we do mean down, with drops in elevation over the first five miles), through the rolling middle distance to the dreaded Newton Hills (Heartbreak Hill, at the twenty-one-mile mark, the most infamous among them), and finally down the homestretch, now forever fraught, on Boylston Street. Qualifying standards were instituted in 1970 and have only become tougher over the years, as competition for a starting bib stiffened (entry to Boston is the lifetime goal of many runners). Perhaps the best measure of how tough the race has become is the median finishing time, about 3:44—the fastest for any annual US marathon.

If that doesn't convince you that you're better off watching than running, how about this: On Marathon Mondays, the Red Sox play at Fenway at eleven a.m. That leaves you time after the game to complete a rare bucket list double dip by joining the crowds in Copley Square cheering runners past the painted pavement of Boston's finish line.

Long before the bombing in 2013 added a layer of significance, the homestretch on Boylston Street was hallowed ground for marathoners.

COLLEGE HOOPS DOUBLEHEADER

WHERE: *Madison Square Garden, New York City*
WHEN: *December to February*

WHY: OVER THE COURSE OF A YEAR, THE MARQUEE OF THE world's most famous arena hawks everything from the Ringling Bros. and Barnum & Bailey Circus to the sideshow that has passed for Knicks teams in this century, but the great tradition of basketball doubleheaders, long a staple of big venues in basketball hotbeds like New York, have gone the way of the flip phone. Until recently, that is.

These days, "NBA Doubleheader" is just a network TV term to describe back-to-back telecasts from different cities. But it used to mean one ticket to see four teams in two games on the same court, one after the other. The idea originated with the Hall of Fame basketball promoter Ned Irish, who in 1934 persuaded the brass at Madison Square Garden that they could sell a lot of tickets and attract top out-of-town teams to face the strong local schools if the games were staged as twin bills. It was a blockbuster idea. Garden doubleheaders sold roughly half a million tickets per season throughout the 1940s, until the point-shaving scandal of 1951 put a damper on the college game. As recently as the 1960s, though, the NBA, still eager to showcase the pro game, staged doubleheaders at the Garden and in other arenas around the league.

It wasn't scandal but the shifting economics of the NBA that put an end to those double dips. Now, though, it's colleges that are reviving the tradition, and you'll find top-flight twin bills at arenas from Los Angeles to Boston. But if you want to go back to where it all started, you can't beat a college doubleheader at the Garden.

Mascots and their teams converge for the Big East tournament at the Garden—part of a revival of the great tradition of college doubleheaders.

SANTA ANITA DERBY

WHERE: *Santa Anita Park, Arcadia, California*
WHEN: *April*

WHY: THIS 1¼-MILE, MILLION-DOLLAR TEST OF TOP three-year-olds often yields not just the Kentucky Derby favorite but the horse that actually wins at Churchill Downs. Ten horses have won both the Santa Anita and Kentucky Derbies, I'll Have Another (2012) and California Chrome (2014) being the most recent to complete that Derby Double. But even if Santa Anita doesn't give you a sure thing to bet on in that other derby, it never fails to deliver the world's most beautiful racing, played out before the cinematic backdrop of the San Gabriel Mountains.

Like so much else in LA, Santa Anita looks incredibly young for her age. It opened on Christmas Day in 1934, the first racetrack in the state. With its distinctive pastel color scheme and its sleek art deco architecture, the place was stylish from the start and a financial winner right out of the gate. Glamorous Hollywood faces became a regular part of the racing crowd—movie mogul Hal Roach was one of the original partners in the track, and stars such as Betty Grable, Lana Turner, Bing Crosby, and Cary Grant were familiar faces there.

All these years later, Santa Anita looks so good that it oughta be in pictures—and sure enough, it often is, showing up on the big screen and TV, in everything from the Marx Brothers' *A Day at the Races* to *Seabiscuit*. So if you experience a powerful sense of déjà vu as you take a seat on Santa Anita Derby Day and look across the track at the mountains, it's probably because you've seen it before, even if you've never been there.

The scene on Derby Day at Santa Anita is racing heaven, even when the winner there doesn't go on to greater glory in the Triple Crown. .

DALLAS COWBOYS AT HOME

WHERE: *AT&T Stadium, Arlington, Texas*
WHEN: *September through December*

WHY: THE DALLAS COWBOYS' HOME IS LIKE A LOT OF HOMES you visit these days: it's sleek and modern, and the first thing you notice is how big the TV is. At AT&T Stadium, we're talking Texas big, 160 by 72 (feet, that is). Ultra-high-def, of course. Sit there among a sellout crowd—because the Cowboys always sell out, and have done so for roughly two hundred games in a row (going back to Texas Stadium)—with the game simultaneously on the field and overhead, and you will hardly believe what you see.

The Cowboys haven't won a Super Bowl in more than twenty years and never regained the dominance they once enjoyed, first in the 1970s (five Super Bowl appearances, two championships, an NFL-best 105 wins), then in the 1990s (three more Super Bowl wins)—and yet the franchise has grown, by some accounts, into the most valuable sports property in the world (worth $4 billion, the last time Forbes checked). They still sport their old nickname, America's Team, but the Cowboys are an international brand, with corporate sponsorship deals unequaled in the NFL, an unwavering fan base, and unflagging attendance at their $1.3-billion home (which means at least the 80,000 listed capacity of AT&T, though 105,121 somehow squeezed in for the Cowboys' first game there in 2009).

They might not run roughshod over the league the way they once did, but their hands-on owner never stops trying, and he makes damn sure none of his efforts goes unnoticed. And the Cowboys still put on one hell of a show, on the field and in their massive close-ups in HD.

Double vision is an option at AT&T, where the action on the field appears simultaneously (but greatly magnified) on 160' x 72' screens.

LA QUEBRADA CLIFF DIVERS

WHERE: *Acapulco, Mexico*
WHEN: *Four times a day, weather permitting*

WHY: THE ROCKY CLIFFS OF LA QUEBRADA SERVE AS THE launchpad for a team of professional divers who plunge, solo or in tandem, into the roiling waters of a narrow gulch 115 feet below. Watching these graceful swan dives and back dives and perfect flips—in the pike position, for all you diving fans—will take your breath away; you can only imagine what it does to theirs.

It's unfortunate, in a way, that Guinness World Records refers to this feat as the highest headfirst dive regularly performed anywhere in the world, which makes it sound like juggling fishbowls or walking on red-hot coals—a mere stunt. But watch the clavadistas of old Acapulco, and you will immediately appreciate both the athleticism and the courage required to survive the rock climbing that precedes every 115-foot dive and the whitecap swimming that follows. For comparison's sake, consider the average high dive at your local swimming pool, then imagine multiplying everything—the height, the speed of descent, the impact with the water—by a factor of ten. Now consider the target that must be hit after spending roughly three seconds in accelerating free fall: in La Quebrada, it's a narrow channel that varies in depth from about six to sixteen feet depending on the wind and the tide. If you hit the water wrong (or hit it at the wrong moment, with the waves rolling out), pity your head and neck, and maybe your spine. The danger and attendant thrill are hardly diminished by the astounding fact that no diver has ever been killed in action here.

With apparent ease and perfect form, La Quebrada's divers throw caution to the wind, aiming for the shallow, churning water 115 feet below.

OPENING DAY IN CINCINNATI

WHERE: *Great American Ball Park, Cincinnati, Ohio*
WHEN: *Opening Day, every year (April 2, 2018)*

WHY: NO SPORT HONORS TRADITION MORE THAN BASEBALL does, and according to one of baseball's oldest traditions, the Cincinnati Reds always play the first game of each new season, and always at home. With the exception of two rainouts (in 1880 and 1966), that tradition held sway for more than a hundred years, and since 1920, the Opening Day game in the Queen City has been preceded by a full-scale parade and daylong festivities that continue even as crowds fill the ballpark.

Of course, Opening Day is not just a mark on the calendar to highlight the launch of thirty teams into a new 162-game orbit; it's a state of mind, a day of hope and renewal, of fresh starts and 0-0 records. It's also a day for skipping school or calling in sick to work so you can watch the game—except in Cincy, where everyone knows it's a holiday.

In baseball, as in so much else in sports these days, TV trumps tradition, but even as Major League Baseball began in the 1990s to schedule games for ESPN to televise the night before the season's official start, it observed tradition in the breach, often saving the designation "Opening Day" for an afternoon game, usually on a Monday in Cincinnati's Riverfront Stadium, the Reds' old park and the site of thirty-two straight openers until the debut of the aptly named Great American Ball Park in 2003. This is where the parade still ends and—for traditionalists, at least—where the new season really begins.

According to baseball tradition, the new season begins with a parade to the ballpark in Cincinnati, where the Reds always open at home.

WARS BETWEEN THE STATES

WHERE: *Various college arenas*
WHEN: *November to March*

WHY: THE GREAT RIVALRIES IN COLLEGE HOCKEY match up well, as they say, with those in any other sport, foreign or domestic, amateur or professional. The best fall into a couple of major categories, and any one deserves a check on your bucket list. After all, as far as the players are concerned, these games are for all the chips.

For starters, you've got your classic intrastate smackdowns, ancient feuds that are carried from one generation to the next, aggravated by proximity. One such classic pits the Seawolves of Alaska Anchorage against the Nanooks of Alaska Fairbanks, a contest known for a legendary pregame bench-clearing brawl precipitated by a vicious hit on a mascot. There are many other worthy in-state rivalries: Michigan vs. Michigan State, an ongoing cold war between teams that have won a combined 12 NCAA titles. There's Boston University vs. Boston College (10 combined titles), Michigan Tech vs. Northern Michigan (4), Denver vs. Colorado College (9), and numerous others, all elite college hockey clashes with extra passion included at no additional charge.

Finally, there are the border wars between schools in adjacent states, and some of the best involve Minnesota, a perennial collegiate power beset on both sides by strong rivals: Wisconsin to the right (the Badgers are five-time NCAA champs, like the Gophers) and North Dakota to the left (the Fighting Sioux have seven titles of their own). These games get a little chippy at times, and the whole scene is reminiscent of Slap Shot—which is precisely why you want to be the building for any of these matches.

Local rivalries in college hockey, whether across shared borders or within them, are charged with passion that equals those in any sport.

THE PALIO DI SIENA

WHERE: *Piazza del Campo, Siena, Italy*
WHEN: *July 2 and August 16*

WHY: HELD ANNUALLY SINCE 1656, THE PALIO DI SIENA IS A feast of pageantry, horsemanship, and bloodcurdling competition, as bareback riders representing ten districts of Siena gallop through hairpin turns around the city's central plaza in a mad dash for honor and bragging rights.

For an event with deep ecclesiastical roots—it began as a celebration of various miraculous manifestations of the Virgin Mary—the Palio has come a very long way. Roughly 35,000 seats fill every available space around, along, and above the track, and another 28,000 spectators jam into the plaza. But that's not nearly enough room to accommodate the crowds, so get there a couple of days early.

The race itself, which is run twice each year and lasts about a minute and a half, is the culmination of four days of spectacle: parades under coats of arms and other displays of medieval pomp and splendor that draw swarms of visitors each year from all over the world. Ten of the city's seventeen districts (or contradas) are entered in the race—the seven that didn't compete in the previous Palio, plus three others drawn by lot. The horses are mixed breeds— no Thoroughbreds allowed—but the competition is pure: three laps around Siena's plaza, no holds barred. The jockeys have no saddles but can use their whips as they see fit; alliances of convenience and ancient feuds are all in play. Safety measures amount to a layer of fresh soil on the track and a little padding along the walls of the most dangerous turns. Unseated riders are not uncommon. Think *Seabiscuit* meets *Game of Thrones*.

The Palio is a contest of breakneck horsemanship, a race that's been running for 350 years on the power of neighborhood bragging rights.

PAWTUCKET SOX AT McCOY FIELD

WHERE: *Pawtucket, Rhode Island*
WHEN: *April through August*

WHY: HOME OF BOSTON'S TRIPLE-A FARM CLUB, THE Pawtucket Red Sox, McCoy, a typical (if charmingly ramshackle) minor-league ballpark, was the site of the longest game in baseball history: thirty-three innings, the Paw Sox vs. the Rochester Red Wings.

The first pitch of that epic was thrown not long after dusk on April 18, 1981, with 1,740 fans in attendance. And though the teams hadn't broken a 2–2 tie after thirty-two innings, and all but a few customers had long since fled the frigid wind (which helped account for the punchless offense and led the players to burn broken bats and sections of the bleachers for warmth), play was suspended at four a.m.

The game was historic, and not only because it was endless. It included two young players who would end up in Cooperstown: Wade Boggs (Pawtucket) and Cal Ripken Jr. (Rochester). Additionally, there were twenty-three others on their way up to or down from the majors, and many more who were stuck in the minors, or so it seemed, forever. It was, in short, a perfect microcosm of minor-league baseball.

As you'd imagine, records were set that stand to this day (most and longest this and that: at-bats, strikeouts, innings pitched), but besides the remarkable cast of characters who played that night (and on June 23, when Rochester returned and Pawtucket won, 3–2), the best thing to come out of the game was Dan Barry's prizewinning book *Bottom of the 33rd,* which the *New York Times* called "a worthy companion to Roger Kahn's classic *Boys of Summer.*" The game and the book made McCoy a shrine to which every true fan must make a pilgrimage.

Home to Boston's Triple-A farm and the site of the longest game in history, McCoy is a perfect window on the world of minor league ball.

WESTMINSTER DOG SHOW

WHERE: *Madison Square Garden, New York City*
WHEN: *February*

WHY: WESTMINSTER IS NOT JUST THE BIGGEST, BADDEST dog show on earth; it's also a "benched" show, which means spectators are free to wander behind the scenes, where they can see the dogs and their owners let their hair down—or fluff it up—as they primp and prep for their brief moment in the ring.

So it has always been at the Westminster Kennel Club Dog Show, and that's a very long time indeed. By some lights, Westminster is neck and neck with the Kentucky Derby as the longest continuously running American sporting event. (Never mind, for the moment, whether the resolve to stage contests in-volving overbred dogs or horses at the peak of World War II, for instance, is something to brag about.) Westminster was the brainchild of a group of New York sporting gents who used to get together to swap tales about hunting and dogs. They incorporated as the Westminster Kennel Club and held their first Bench Show for Dogs in 1877. It was an immediate hit and only grew in size and stature. By 1926, the show took up annual residence in Madison Square Garden. By 1948 it was on TV, which has never put a dent in the live gate at the Garden.

Nothing can keep the dog crowd away—certainly not the fact that the most popular US breeds, Labs and Goldens, have never won Westminster. Even the losers are a miracle of composure and competence in the ring. And backstage, as they're fussed over by handlers and gawked at by strangers, the forbearance and good temper of these dogs make it obvious why humans have loved and fed them since we stood up and walked on our own hind legs.

All the preparation and primping paid off for C.J. (above), a German shorhaired pointer, who was "Best in Show" in 2016.

THE DODGERS AT CHAVEZ RAVINE

WHERE: *Los Angeles, California*
WHEN: *April to September*

WHY: WHEN THE BROOKLYN DODGERS MOVED WEST before the 1958 season, the promise of a glorious new stadium was a powerful part of the lure. That ballpark opened in April 1962, which makes it the third-oldest in the majors, after Fenway and Wrigley, and, like those antiques, Dodger Stadium is still a treasure.

Even when we call it Chavez Ravine, we tend to forget that nickname comes from the Mexican American neighborhood that stood in its place before its displaced residents were forced to sell under eminent domain to make room for planned public housing. A turn of political tides in LA washed away the housing plan, and—lo and behold!—the vacant land was soon reacquired by the city and made available to the Dodgers' owner, Walter O'Malley, who had failed to get the new stadium he wanted from Brooklyn.

The Dodgers and their stadium—privately financed, it must be said—were an immediate and rousing success in LA, and so they remained. They won the World Series in 1959 and have added eight NL pennants and four more Series wins since their ballpark opened. Inside and outside the white lines, Dodger Stadium is spacious: a pitcher's park with MLB's largest capacity (56,000), it's a perennial attendance leader. And no wonder the fans turn out. As you gaze across the outfield at the San Gabriel Mountains beyond, the wavy, angled roofline, so familiar from iconic photos of Hall of Fame Dodgers hurlers—from Koufax and Drysdale to Sutton and Valenzuela—is a constant reminder that you're sitting in a historic park that remains one of the best places on earth to watch a ballgame.

The new stadium that helped lure the Dodgers to LA was an immediate hit and still is among the best places to see a ballgame.

THE HIGHLAND GAMES

WHERE: *Dunoon, Scotland*
WHEN: *August*

WHY: SOME OF THE STRENGTH COMPETITIONS AT COWAL Highland Gathering in Dunoon, the largest Scottish games in Great Britain, seem like the ancient versions of modern field events, but on steroids. That might be hard to wrap your head around, since athletes in modern field events themselves have so often been on steroids, but you'll get the idea right away at the events they call "heavy athletics": the objects to be tossed or flung or hurled or flipped are enormous, and so are the athletes. It's like watching the guys from *Braveheart* at recess.

Indeed, some accounts trace the origins of these games to the eleventh century or even earlier, where they were said to demonstrate some of the strengths and skills useful to men in their everyday labors. It is said, too, that a display about the Highland games at the 1889 Paris Exposition influenced the inventor of the modern Olympics, Baron Pierre de Coubertin, when he was planning his modern reinvention of the games.

The connections are plain to see: the stone put and hammer throw are like the Olympic shot put and hammer, but with heavier weights (26-pound shots and up to 56-pound hammers, versus the sixteen 16-pounders used in both events nowadays). But the most awe-inspiring test, by far, is the caber toss. This requires each competitor to lift something resembling a tapered telephone pole—about 20 feet long and maybe 175 pounds—narrow-end down, then heave it, end over end, so it lands, fat-end down, at a perfect vertical. It is said the caber toss evolved from the need to transport the beams for buildings across the brooks and streams of the Scottish Highlands. As best we can tell, though, this event has no analog in the modern Olympics.

The Highland Games often look like modern field events on steroids, especially the caber toss, in which big men flip huge poles end over end.

YALE VS. PRINCETON

WHERE: *The Yale Bowl, New Haven, Connecticut*
WHEN: *November, even numbered years*

WHY: THE TEAMS FROM THESE TWO AUGUST INSTITUTIONS did not meet in the first college football game (that would've been Princeton vs. Rutgers in 1869), but the Bulldogs' annual meeting with the Tigers reprises one of the oldest rivalries in American sports and probably the oldest in college football. The teams first met in 1873, and have done so 139 times since.

College football might not have been invented at Princeton, but there were reportedly guys with orange-striped sleeves at the Creation. And the so-called Father of American Football, Walter Camp, played and coached at Yale. These two schools dominated early intercollegiate competition, winning virtually all of the first forty national titles, between 1869 and 1904 (retroactively awarded). As football spread and competition intensified through the first half of the twentieth century, the relative strength of the Ivy League diminished. But by then Yale and Princeton had made an indelible mark on football—on the game and on the culture it spawned.

Consider these two not entirely random facts: (1) The Yale Bowl, opened in 1914, was the first bowl-shaped football stadium in the United States; it inspired the design and name of the Rose Bowl and countless other stadiums, from which postseason "bowl" games derive their names. (2) These two teams played in what was apparently the first game ever captured on film, when Thomas Edison pointed his newfangled motion-picture camera (he called it the Kinetograph) at the action in 1903, giving us the earliest foretaste of a world dominated and transfixed by screens bearing moving images of football.

They didn't play the very first college game, but these rivals have been going at it since 1873 and have greatly influenced the sport's evolution.

COLLEGE WORLD SERIES

WHERE: *TD Ameritrade Park, Omaha, Nebraska*
WHEN: *June*

WHY: THE NCAA DIVISION 1 CHAMPIONSHIP, A.K.A. the College World Series (CWS), is like the kid brother of pro baseball, and its early appeal stemmed from precisely those qualities that were not major league. The venue, for instance, was Rosenblatt Stadium, a charming ballpark of minor-league proportions and the home of the CWS since its inception in 1950. Then there were the baby-faced teams wearing those fantastic bush-league uniforms, and that unmistakable ping of metal bats.

But little brother grew up: ESPN began broadcasting CWS games in 1982 and has shown every game of the tournament since 2003. Rosenblatt Field was replaced by TD Ameritrade Park Omaha. The bats still ping, but a sure sign of maturity is the fact that alcohol was on sale to all patrons (not just those in premium seats) in 2016—the first time it's been permitted at any NCAA championship.

While the CWS was coming of age, it also became a major source of big-league talent. Roughly 60 percent of MLB draft picks in this century have played college ball. In one five-year stretch, for instance, four of the number one picks were college kids, from David Price (2007) to Gerrit Cole (2011), with Bryce Harper and Stephen Strasburg in between. The overall number one pick in 2016, Dansby Swanson, of Vanderbilt, had announced himself to the wider world in two straight CWS appearances. All of which explains why Omaha is the go-to destination for fans who want a glimpse of tomorrow's stars while they are still college kids, playing baseball for the pure joy of it—and, of course, for a shot at the glory.

It hasn't quite reached March Madness proportions, but this tournament has grown into a talent-rich, 64-team baseball extravaganza.

THE DAWG POUND

WHERE: *FirstEnergy Stadium, Cleveland, Ohio*
WHEN: *Sundays, autumn*

WHY: HIGH ON ANY LIST OF MANIAC FANS ARE THE DENIZENS of the bleachers behind the east end zone at Cleveland Browns home games. This is the Dawg Pound, the pack of rabid fans whose notoriety since 1985 has only spurred them on to more extreme and outlandish costumes and behavior.

Perhaps the most important question to ponder before you pay an anthropological visit to the Dawg Pound is this: If you were a Browns fan, wouldn't you be a little crazy, too? Soon after the Dawgs' advent, the Browns became an almost ceaseless example of ineptitude on the field that reflected chaos and incompetence in the front office. Is it any wonder that the fans gaze back longingly at the 1950s (three NFL titles) or even the 1980s (seven post-season appearances)? Could it be that the Browns' elegant logo-less helmets that are so appealingly retro are actually the marketing department's subtle reminder of those good old days?

And yet there is always hope—or its ungodly spawn—on display in the Dawg Pound. New owners took over the Browns in 2012, and immediate changes were made. Then more changes, and more after that. In 2016, the team switched football leadership for the fourth time in, well, four years, hiring the baseball analytics legend Paul DePodesta (played by Jonah Hill in the movie *Moneyball*) as chief strategy officer, and Hue Jackson as the new coach. An entirely new draft strategy and other major personnel changes ensued, and hope was rekindled in the Dawg Pound, where, as ever, the famous chant could be heard: *Here we go, Brownies, here we go! Woof, woof!*

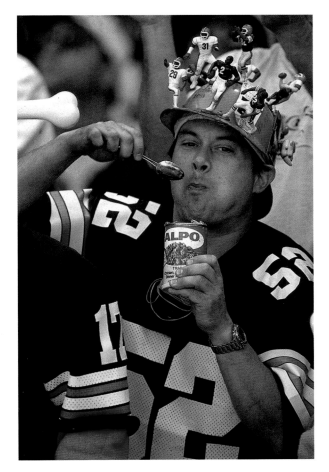

Since they came to fame in the mid-eighties, the rabid fans in the Dawg Pound have had more bark than the Browns have had bite.

AUSSIE FOOTBALL GRAND FINAL

WHERE: *Melbourne Cricket Ground, Melbourne, Australia*
WHEN: *Last Saturday in September (or first in October)*

WHY: AUSTRALIAN-RULES FOOTBALL IS A FIERCE COUSIN OF many run-and-kick sports—a fast-paced, high-scoring, full-contact melee pitting teams of eighteen players in a contest that seems like yet another expression of man's basic evolutionary need to run through fields in packs, pursuing a ball and hitting people.

They've been playing the game since 1897 in the Victorian (now Australian) Football League. Its closest relative might be Gaelic football, except Aussie rules is professional, unlike its Irish cousin, and it's played with an oval ball (not a round one, like Gaelic) on an oval field (not a rectangular one). Also, full tackling is not just allowed in footy, but encouraged. The game resembles rugby, but it's more free-flowing, without all those tedious scrums. It's like American football, too, but it's played in shorts and T-shirts, without pads or headgear; and it's a bit like hockey, if only in the tendency toward fisticuffs (YouTube is knee deep in footy's greatest hits—highlight reels of fights and crippling flying tackles). In short, it's a barrel of laughs, which might explain its growing popularity over the past twenty years in Oceania and parts of Asia.

The Grand Final is the culmination of a month-long playoff series involving the top eight teams in the Australian Football League, the winner of which is crowned "the premiers." The league's games draw big crowds throughout the regular season (averaging almost 40,000), and the Grand Final is Australia's biggest sporting event, reliably selling out the enormous Melbourne Cricket Ground and drawing more than 100,000 fans. In a country that loves its sports, the Aussie-rules Grand Final is now king.

The appeal of footy was apparent in the 2013 grand final: full-contact action with no pads, the Blues vs. the Lions for all the marbles.

PRO FOOTBALL HALL OF FAME GAME

WHERE: *Tom Benson Hall of Fame Field, Canton, Ohio*
WHEN: *First full weekend in August*

WHY: THIS IS THE FIRST CHANCE FOR NFL FANS TO BREAK their enforced six-month football fast with the kick-off of the NFL preseason, but it's also a great opportunity to observe the convergence of the pro game at its mythmaking best (as only a hall of fame can glorify it) and the stark reality of what numbers on a program—e.g., "six-foot-eight, three hundred forty-five pounds"—mean up close, in the flesh.

Consider the game, which follows the annual Saturday induction ceremonies: the first taste of football after the off-season is always sweet, even if it's an exhibition. And it's all the better at the Hall of Fame Stadium, which is redolent of history (Marion Motley scored the first touchdown at the stadium as a high school player, eight years before he broke the color barrier in modern pro football with the Browns in '46). The field is still the home to several local high school teams, so it's small enough for you to get a true sense of the scale of the players, something that is simply impossible on TV from the upper deck of a huge NFL dome. No matter where your seat is in Canton, walk down to field level once the players emerge, because their sheer size, no matter how well you know their vital stats, will be a revelation.

Remember, too, that you are in Canton, where pro football was born, and it's Hall of Fame Weekend, an officially sanctioned time to immerse yourself in the game's lore and legend. The hall, which opened in 1963 as a pint-sized two-room roadside attraction, has grown into a 55,000-square-foot colossus. And for most NFL fans, its unalloyed celebration of the game, its heroes and its values, is mother's milk for the football soul.

After fans get their first taste of the season ahead at the annual Hall of Fame game in Canton, a feast of football history awaits at the hall itself.

ELEPHANT POLO CHAMPIONSHIP

WHERE: *Meghauli, Nepal*
WHEN: *November*

WHY: THIS IS A VARIATION OF THE GAME PLAYED ON horseback, but with elephants instead of horses, two people aboard each four-ton beast, one to steer and control the animal, the other to whack at a polo ball with a six- to ten-foot bamboo mallet and score goals. Nothing to it.

The game was invented by two Brits in Nepal and has attracted teams from Sri Lanka, India, and Thailand (among other places). Just showing up for this event takes enormous desire: to get to Balia National Park, where the championships are held, players must endure a two-hour bus ride after a forty-minute flight in a small plane—from Kathmandu, that is, which is about as far from London as you can get on this planet.

Though under steady attack in recent years by PETA and other animal-protection activists—who have at times succeeded in disrupting the schedule of the competition—elephant polo's ground-shaking world championship tournament has been staged annually in Nepal since 1982. The organizers and supporters of the game point to the conservation of endangered animals (chiefly, Asian elephants, tigers, and rhinos) and their habitat as one of their chief goals and the beneficiary of their charity, so the clash of elephants on a pitch is not the only bitterly fought contest on offer at these championships. Talk about a Rumble in the Jungle! Somewhere in the world you might find action that's faster than elephants chasing polo balls, but in terms of sheer tonnage in motion, you will never beat these World Championships.

It's an earthshaking event when teams of four-ton animals with two men aboard chase a ball around, whacking at it with mallets.

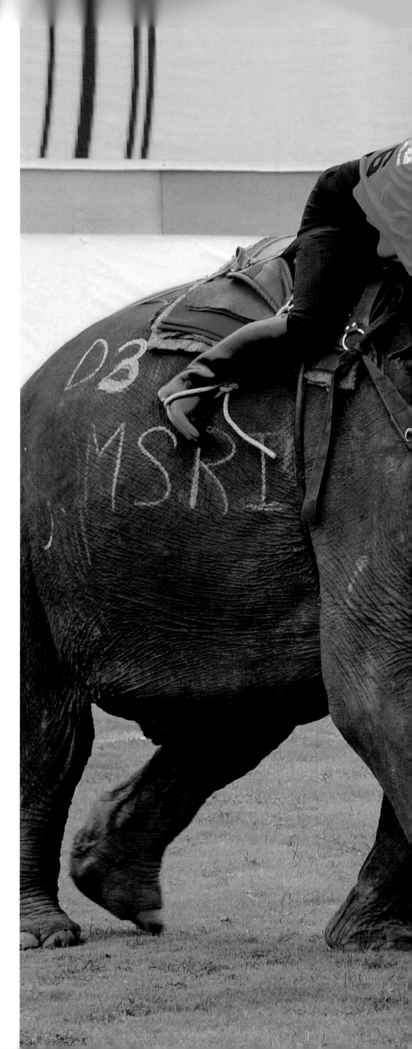

PAULEY PAVILION

WHERE: *University of California, Los Angeles, California*
WHEN: *November to March*

WHY: AFTER THE BRUINS WON THEIR FIRST NATIONAL championship in 1964, what had long been apparent to coach John Wooden was obvious to all: the men's gym at UCLA, an ancient 1,500-seat firetrap widely known as the B.O. Barn, needed an upgrade. Pauley Pavilion opened the next year and hosted the greatest run of domination in basketball history—ten NCAA titles in twelve years, including seven in a row (a mark still unchallenged in the men's game, though recently surpassed by UConn's women). The new arena may have been named for Edwin Pauley, a principal contributor to its funding, but it was Wooden and his teams who made it a landmark.

In truth, the legend of Bruins basketball was already beginning to take shape by the time the inaugural game was played at Pauley. That first contest featured Wooden's prize recruit, Lew Alcindor, playing for the freshman team against the Bruins varsity squad, who happened to be the reigning national champions and the preseason number one. The freshman won by fifteen points, heralding a bright future.

Exactly how bright could've hardly been imagined at the time. Until his retirement in 1975, Wooden embedded excellence in Bruins basketball and set standards of achievement that seem impossible to match. In the next forty years (through 2016), nine coaches followed, and UCLA won more than 70 percent of its games, adding one national championship banner to the collection Wooden left behind. Pauley Pavilion has been renovated, but the basketball is still excellent when the Bruins play there—on a court named for Wooden and his beloved wife, Nell.

Wooden's success at UCLA hasn't been matched in the 40 years since he retired, but the Bruins have been consistent winners in Pauley.

WORLD SERIES OF POKER

WHERE: *Las Vegas, Nevada*
WHEN: *November*

WHY: IT WASN'T LONG AGO THAT POKER WAS JUST A GOOD excuse for a night out with the guys. It was a game, not a spectator sport, and there were no stars, just a few legends: Will Wild Bill Hickok, Amarillo Slim, Doyle Brunson. Were those guys even real? Who knew for sure?

That was before 1970, when a Las Vegas casino owner and poker enthusiast named Benny Binion invited seven of the best-known players in the world to a little game of cards, to be held in public, at his Horseshoe Casino in Las Vegas. He called the tournament—grandiosely, it seemed at the time—the World Series of Poker.

Flash-forward through the birth of the Internet, online gambling, and the poker boom of the early twenty-first century. Now pause for a moment at 2006: Binion's little card game is a gigantic international brand, WSOP!, boasting divisions on five continents and offering online poker to all comers at any hour in any time zone around the globe. The tournament currently encompasses sixty-five major competitions in most variants of poker, but Texas Hold 'Em has long since emerged as the final measure of the best players in the world.

The winner of that 2006 Main Event (as the high-stakes, no-limit Hold 'Em competition is now known) was a guy named Jamie Gold, who took home a record $12 million. The top spot is worth a mere $5 million or so these days, but the total prize money is still upward of $60 million—all of which is what makes this the only poker game you ever really need to see.

What began as a small, invitational poker game has grown into an international giant, with an enormous field and millions at stake.

THE TRAVERS STAKES

WHERE: *Saratoga Race Course, Saratoga Springs, New York*
WHEN: *August*

WHY: HERE'S HOW YOU GET TO SARATOGA FROM NEW YORK City, according to the great sportswriter Red Smith: drive north for about 175 miles, turn left on Union Avenue, and go back one hundred years. For our money (and Red's, apparently), Saratoga is the best racetrack on the planet. And though the calendar is thick with rich stakes and the classy Thoroughbreds they attract, the Grade 1 Travers is the highlight of the Saratoga meeting—the Midsummer Derby, a mile and a quarter on dirt for three-year-olds, just like the one in Kentucky.

They've been racing at Saratoga for more than 150 years, and everything about the place has the feel of an easier age. A good day starts at dawn in the mist of the Oklahoma Training Track, where you can stand at the rail, alongside the horsemen with stopwatches, and recall that thrill you felt the first time you saw a racehorse up close. Later, when the crowds have arrived, the picnic ground behind the grandstand—Saratoga's backyard—is the place to sit under the ancient shade trees and take in the barbecue smells and the fiddle and banjo music in the air.

But it's ultimately the horses that have always drawn the crowds to Saratoga. Most of the great ones have come this way, and many met their match. Man o' War lost for the only time here, to Upset. Among the twelve Triple Crown winners in history, only Whirlaway has gone on to win the Travers. Secretariat and Affirmed and American Pharoah all lost at Saratoga. That's why this place is known as the "Graveyard of Champions." But we like to think of it by another of its nicknames, the one derived from the local hot springs, a place that soothes the body and spirit: the Spa.

Saratoga's splendors are on display from dawn to dusk every August, but the showstopper in 2016, as always, was the Travers winner, Arrogate..

PGA AT THE COLISEUM

WHERE: *TPC Scottsdale, Scottsdale, Arizona*
WHEN: *February*

WHY: THE STADIUM COURSE AT TPC SCOTTSDALE WAS BUILT to host the Phoenix Open, and for the week each year when the PGA Tour stops here, it is the place where the country club and the cheap seats meet.

The idea was to carve a course out of the desert that would be a fitting test for touring pros and could handle the swarms of fans drawn to the spectacle. These goals were realized most apparently on the 16th hole, where the temporary bleachers erected for the tournament each year make this 162-yard par-three the only hole on the PGA Tour surrounded by spectator seating. There is room for 16,000 fans, for whom the usual rules of golf-gallery comportment and etiquette are suspended. Fans do not exchange bon mots in the traditional golf whisper. They boo bad shots as lustily as they cheer good ones. They chant, they adore, they mock, they curse. They sometimes act like drunken frat boys, which many of them, in fact, are.

Things went over the top, though, in 2015, when Francesco Molinari's hole in one was greeted by a celebratory blizzard of beer cans from the gallery that sent players and caddies running for cover and left the green blanketed by hundreds of sudsy missiles. It was at that moment when one could only hope that both the name sponsor and the tournament—the Waste Management Phoenix Open—got what they paid for.

One thing is certain about this course and tournament: the fans love it. Annual attendance holds steady at about 500,000, quite a few of whom can be heard airing their views on the 16th hole.

Golf's rules of decorum don't apply on No. 16 at the Phoenix Open, the only hole on the PGA Tour surrounded by fans, and a scene like no other.

GRAND PRIX OF MONACO

WHERE: *Principality of Monaco*
WHEN: *Sunday of Memorial Day weekend*

WHY: LIKE INDY AND DAYTONA, MONACO TRANSCENDS ITS sport, enjoying a special status in the world at large and conferring that status on every winner. Part of its magic is surely the setting, a Mediterranean resort whose rising, falling, twisting seaside streets are turned over each spring to the best Formula One drivers in the world. Consider the giants who make up the list of repeat winners: Ayrton Senna (six wins), Graham Hill and Michael Schumacher (five each), Alain Prost (four), and Jackie Stewart and Stirling Moss (three).

What really sets this race apart, though, is the course itself—a demanding two-mile circuit along coastal mountainsides, through a tunnel and a series of hairpin turns, with a couple of brief straightaways thrown in for fun. It requires precise driving and intense concentration, not to mention sheer guts, throughout its seventy-eight laps. Until Armco barriers were installed along much of the course beginning in 1969, drivers who left the racing surface simply crashed into whatever was along the Monaco roadside.

But let's be perfectly honest: you don't have to know Formula One from Vicks Formula 44 to want to spend the week in Monaco in the spring. Imagine a little strip of paradise along the French Riviera; now picture a casino where James Bond would feel right at home with Honey Ryder on one arm and Pussy Galore on the other. Now throw in the couple-dozen incredibly cool Formula One cars turned loose every afternoon on the streets of Monaco, from Thursday's practice right through Grand Prix racing on Sunday. Now, quick: name a place you'd rather be spending Memorial Day weekend. Go ahead. We're waiting.

The seaside streets of Monaco are turned over to the world's best drivers for three days of practice, then for a little Formula One racing.

LE CLUB DE HOCKEY CANADIEN

WHERE: *Bell Centre, Montreal, Canada*
WHEN: *October to February*

WHY: THE CANADIENS ARE NOT JUST ONE OF THE NHL'S Original Six, but the only remaining team that actually predates the formation of the league. The Habs played their home games for seven decades at the Montreal Forum, which from 1926 to 1995 was the seat of a dynasty that reigned over the world of hockey, winning more Stanley Cups (twenty-four) than any other team.

When the action shifted in 1996 to the Bell Centre (at that time called the Molson Centre), the Canadiens brought along plenty of decorations for the new place. Hanging from the rafters at Cana-diens games are fifteen jerseys bearing the retired numbers of the great players who helped win those twenty-four Stanley Cups. The championship banners hang there, too, tokens of the era when the darlings of francophone Canada enjoyed sustained dominion in the NHL. The Habs—their nickname comes from *habitants*, the early French settlers of Canada—won at least five cups in three straight decades (the fifties, sixties, and seventies), including five in a row from 1956 to 1960.

What followed was, by Canadiens standards, a long period of mediocrity (a single NHL title in the eighties and one last cup at the Forum, in '93). Since the move to the Bell Centre, they've advanced as far as the conference finals only once. You'd think that twenty years into an era of relatively middling hockey, the Habs would be an easy ticket in Montreal, right? Not exactly. Their average attendance every year is 21,288, which happens to be the capacity at Bell. Every Canadiens game is a sellout.

The jerseys and banners that hang in the Bell Centre are tokens of an era when Rocket Richard (above) and a Habs dynasty ruled the NHL.

BASEBALL BY THE BAY

WHERE: *AT&T Park, San Francisco, California*
WHEN: *April through September*

WHY: THE SITE OF BARRY BONDS' NOW-INFAMOUS march to hallowed home run records, and more recently of the Giants' three World Series triumphs, AT&T Park (the former Pacific Bell Park) stands hard by McCovey Cove, where so many of Bonds' titanic blasts over the twenty-four-foot right field wall—known locally as "splash hits"—were fished from the drink by a flotilla of fanatical souvenir seekers.

But you don't have to be a crazed seamhead—hell, you don't even have to particularly like baseball—to be enthralled by the scene at AT&T. Although it opened way back in 2000, replacing the notoriously frigid and windblown Candlestick Park, the Giants' home remains a part of any serious conversation about the best ballparks in the majors. It's not just the consistently good sightlines that distinguish this place—there actually might not be a bad seat in the house—or the breathtaking views of the bay, the Bay Bridge, and Oakland beyond. It's not just the conspicuously friendly staff or the high-end ballpark food (where else would you dare order a ballpark crab sandwich or the porcini doughnuts and not regret it?). And it's not just the knowledgeable and highly partisan crowd (though their vibe is more We Love Our Giants than We're a Torch Mob and We're Coming for You Out-of-Towners, which you find in certain precincts of, say, the Bronx or Philadelphia). It's all of those things, plus the exceptional quality of the baseball, that explains why the Giants have drawn three million fans and have sold more than 99 percent of the tickets to all home games over the past five seasons.

In place of the frigid misery of Candlestick, AT&T offers comfort and perhaps the majors' best views—and, lately, some of the best baseball.

THE LEWISTON COLISÉE

WHERE: *Lewiston, Maine*
WHEN: *December to February*

WHY: THIS LITTLE NEW ENGLAND ARENA, AND THE BACKDROP for perhaps the most famous sports photograph ever taken, will go down in history as the scene of one of the great upsets since David turned a slingshot on Goliath—Muhammad Ali's first-round knockout of Sonny Liston in their 1965 heavyweight title rematch. The place is still open for business, hosting hockey games as it did more than sixty years ago when, still known as the Central Maine Youth Center, it was suddenly the center of the sports universe.

The historic fight was as brief as the buildup to it was protracted, though the controversy surrounding it will probably never die. Ali knocked Liston to the canvas less than two minutes into the first round. After rising to one knee, Liston tumbled onto his back and was counted out at 2:12 into the fight. Depending on whom you ask, the right hand that KO'd Liston was either incredibly quick and lethal or it was a "phantom punch," after which Liston took a dive. What is certain is that Ali stood over Liston, screaming at him to get up and fight, and in that instant, Neil Leifer, perfectly positioned, snapped a photograph as iconic as any sports picture ever taken. Liston would eventually mount a comeback, winning eleven fights, but never getting another title shot. Ali would become what he had long since called himself, the Greatest, and much of the world would come to agree.

These days, the place where it all happened is home to the Fighting Spirit of the North American 3 Hockey League, a developmental and showcase league for aspiring college players and pros. Lest we forget, youth hockey was why this nifty little arena was built in the first place, and it made possible the fight that launched the Ali era, in sports and beyond.

Now called the Colisée and used mainly for hockey, this is where Ali KO'd Liston, launching an era and producing the most iconic of sports images.

ACKNOWLEDGMENTS

This book would not have been possible if we hadn't had the good fortune to spend decades working at *Sports Illustrated*—and not just any decades, but those that coincided with the golden age of magazines. If you loved sports and you loved telling stories in print, there was no better place to work than *SI*. So to Mark Mulvoy, who hired us both, and to his successors at *SI*—John Papanek, Bill Colson, and Terry McDonell—we owe a huge debt. We are grateful, as well, to the photographers whose work brings these pages to life, and to Dot McMahon, Carolyn Davis, and Jake Traub, who gathered thousands upon thousands of images for us to choose from. Thanks, too, to Heloisa Zero for her expertise at the delicate point where design and technology converge. Before he went off to tame the Wild West, Dave Hirshey championed this book at Harper Collins, where he himself was the champ. There, he left us in the good hands of Marta Schooler, Rebecca Hunt, and Lynne Yeamans, and with the unwavering friendship and support of Michael Morrison. And, of course, nothing we do would be complete—or even worth starting—without the incomparable Esther Newberg and our insurmountable home-field advantage: Suzanne Noli and Marilyn Johnson.

THE SPORTS BUCKET LIST

Copyright © 2017 by Low Gear and Minus, Inc.
and Apartment 8H Inc.

HarperCollins books may be purchased for educational, business, or sales promotional use. For information please email the Special Markets Department at SPsales@harpercollins.com.

Published in 2017 by
Harper Design
An Imprint of HarperCollins*Publishers*
195 Broadway
New York, NY 10007
Tel: (212) 207-7000
Fax: (855) 746-6023
harperdesign@harpercollins.com
www.hc.com

Distributed throughout the world by
HarperCollins *Publishers*
195 Broadway
New York, NY 10007

ISBN 978-0-06-257217-2
Library of Congress Control Number: 2016952299
Printed in China
First Printing, 2017